12MONTHS IN THE SADDLE

First published by Carlton Books Ltd in 2013
Carlton Books Ltd,
20 Mortimer Street
London W1T 3JW

10 9 8 7 6 5 4 3 2 1

Text and pictures © John Deering and Phil Ashley
Design © Carlton Books Ltd

A CIP catalogue record for this book is available from the British Library.

ISBN 978-1-78097-294-7

Printed and bound in Dubai

12MONTHS IN THE SADDLE

THE STORY OF HOW TWO CYCLISTS TACKLED A DOZEN EPIC RIDES

Foreword by **SEAN YATES**

JOHN DEERING AND **PHIL ASHLEY**

CARLTON

Contents

Sean Yates

Foreword by Sean Yates

I hate to think of how many months I've spent on my bike. I was out around the lanes of Sussex where I grew up as far back as I can remember, then as a young amateur racer I would be bashing out the miles in road races and time trials up and down the country.

I turned professional when I was 21 and went on to ride the Tour de France 12 times in my career. In the 1980s, professionals could find themselves racing for literally half the year with nearly all of the days leftover given up for training.

As a retired bike rider, I have attracted more than my fair share of funny looks and knowing nods from other ex-pros as I have continued to ride my bike wherever and whenever I can. At least when I was a sporting director, I had a ready-made professional excuse for getting out there.

The truth is, I like riding my bike. I always enjoy riding my bike, even when riding my bike isn't enjoyable. Those of you who have battled the elements with thoughts of only a strong cup of tea and a hot bath to guide you home will know exactly what I mean.

And that's what I've got in common with John and Phil. They like riding their bikes too. They get it. Every single one of these 12 rides made me think, "I wouldn't mind doing that." Even the ones I've done many times before. I thought, "I wouldn't mind doing that again." With that in mind, maybe I'll see you out there some time.

Happy riding,

Sean Yates

John Deering

Phil Ashley

Introduction

Cycling, eh? A British Tour de France winner. A British World Champion. The Olympics up Box Hill and round Hampton Court. And a million mamils (middle-aged-men-in-lycra) choking up the country lanes of Britain every Sunday morning.

This book is unashamedly written with love for the mamil. The mamil dreams of weekends away in France, Italy and Belgium. And Sussex. Not frolicking with his family in the soothing warm waters of the Med, or roaring on strippers with colleagues after a trade show in Brussels. No. He wants to walk back into work on Monday morning, cycling shoes clickety-clacking across hard marble floors, throw his bulging bag stuffed with Paul Smith suit on to his chair and announce with a flourish: "This time yesterday morning, I was half way up L'Alpe d'Huez."

This is the story of our 12 months in the saddle. Well, to be more accurate, our one or two days a month in the saddle for 12 months, but that didn't sound quite so snappy. And anyway, somebody has ridden all the way round the world in just over three months, so there wouldn't be anywhere else to go for the other nine, would there?

Our aim was to go and do 12 great bike rides and tell you what it was like. Not in a "turn left here, do a right under the railway bridge," sort of way, but actually what it was like. We wanted to make the rides as varied as possible. Discussing and arguing over which ones we were going to do was as much fun as doing them. In fact at times, especially when we were cold and wet on some hitherto unknown windswept, rain-drenched mountainside, the planning was infinitely more enjoyable. It is easier to drink beer while planning than riding, too.

We've been to Scotland, Wales, France, Belgium and Italy. We've been to the north, west and south of England. We

went the wrong way almost as many times as the right way, but we didn't ask directions once, for we are men.

I do the writing, Phil does the pictures. I do the writing afterwards, which is an advantage that he doesn't get to enjoy, so he rigged up all sorts of sneaky things to have his way. He has a secret battery in one of his bottle cages, for instance, and a remote control button for his camera on the handlebars. He also occasionally gets other people to press the button for him, whereas I do all the words myself. Except for the ones he does, I suppose.

We like to spend a couple of days at each of these things. We ride it, then we go back and shoot it wherever we can. Events like sportives that all happen on one day are a bit trickier, but hell, we manage.

Phil – What John is trying to say is that I do all the technical stuff while he swans around and then writes it all down at his leisure over a pint and a ploughman's. I'm not bitter, though.

He goes uphill quicker than me, but I go downhill quicker than him, so we meet at the bottom. He usually waits for me. At times, I've even waited for him. We're good to each other like that.

If this book inspires you to get your bike out of the garage, great. If it makes you want to go out and do one of these rides yourself, great. If it inspires you to throw it across the room and put X-Factor back on, go ahead. Each to his own.

Whatever you do, remember it's meant to be fun.

January

Coast to Coast

It was one of the first days of the brand new year. I was riding my bike round to Phil's house. It was a blueish-purple Raleigh Tomahawk I'd had for barely more than a week, which had been waiting for me under the Christmas tree when my little brother and I had finally been allowed into the living room. Despite us having been camped outside the door in the hallway for hours, it was still before dawn. And there it was. Like a smaller Chopper, without the gears, perfect for the eight-year-old me.

On this crispy January morning, I had swung right out of the garden gate, bumped along the uneven paving stones of West Way, cut across the muddy football pitch in Crossways Park, then down The Warren. There was an alleyway that linked The Warren to Dorset Waye and Devon Waye, where the Ashleys lived, and also the Taylor twins, Jane and Ruth. I don't suppose kids in 2012 would dream of just pitching up at each other's homes without texting first but hey, these were crazy days. Crazy.

I've later discovered that in Sussex, alleys like this are called twittens, in Oxfordshire they are jitties, and in the North-East this would be a snicket. In Middlesex, as some people still call it, they were just alleys, and this one had a pair of those horizontal bars that you had to wiggle round, positioned to dissuade youths on motorbikes from using them as a short cut. I had already flagrantly ridden past the "No Cycling" sign to get this far. Rebel.

My brain, normally filled with delusional visions that every time I kicked a football there could be a scout from a professional team driving past our garden so I'd better do it right, turned to the possibility of limboing my new Tomahawk under one of those bars. Hell, why not both of them?

Left: Looking west from Whinlatter Pass. The north-west of the Lake District is less busy than the better-known Lakeland tourist traps.

I was no fool. I didn't just race straight up to it. I already knew I could crouch low enough to get my head and the line of my back below the height of the super-cool high-rise handlebars. Offering the bike up to the bar, I demonstrated to myself and any scouts from Billy Smart's Circus who happened to be driving past that the bars and the saddle with backrest and "Not For Passenger Use" sign would just slip with the smallest amount of clearance below the Bar of Death. That was all I needed.

Casually rolling back towards the mouth of the alley, I steeled myself. This was the moment. Visualise your victory, I told myself. Deep breaths. A countdown of three and I was off, smoothly up to a steady pace, then tucking down below the line of the bars, concentrating on keeping the Tomahawk 100 per cent upright, closing upon the steel bar that should be blocking my path but was about to be tricked into letting me through unhindered.

Now, sharper-eyed readers may have noticed that when I had offered the bike up to the bar and found it just squeezed below it, I really should have taken into account the extra width of my fingers on the handlebars. The confident cruise up to the bar was brought to an immediate and excruciating halt by this miscalculation; eight eight-year-old fingers jammed between the handlebar of my bike and the round steel bar.

I can't remember what happened next, as the pain shut out all other thoughts. I do know I didn't tell anybody about it until very recently. It's still not funny.

Phil – *Actually, it is quite funny. I went back to Dorset Waye for a look and those bars are still there, if a little bit worse for wear. A bit like John and his self-delusional ambitions. The pavement has sunk and left the bars at an angle that wouldn't encourage a 2012 kid to try the trick, even if he could bear to leave his*

*X-Box alone for five minutes. I like to believe
I could still make out eight little dents in one
of them, though.*

Thirty-six years later, possibly to the day, I find
myself on the way to Phil's house again. Roughly
halfway between these two dates, he had the
good sense to marry the Jane half of the Taylor
twins, and they got a house of their own not too
far away from our old stomping grounds.

We're on our way to Cumbria and
Northumberland for the weekend to begin our
year-long odyssey by taking on the C2C, Coast
to Coast, or, if you prefer, Sea 2 Sea. That's
what our map calls it, anyway. Snow is forecast,
and by the time the Renault Espace creeps
out of Phil's driveway, it's groaning under the
weight of two road bikes, two mountain bikes,
a lot of cycling kit, a lot of camera kit, and
three middle-aged men of varying size. With
us is Mark, old friend, cameraman and, on this
occasion, photographer's assistant.

By lunchtime, as snow begins to fall, Mark and Phil will be trying to push the Espace up a slip road of the M6 near Warrington, which is where the cam-belt has decided to snap and completely trash the engine.

The Espace is soon on its way back south as a guest of the AA. We three intrepid heroes, however, have shrugged off the misfortune with a wry grin and a manly gesture and are continuing north, this time in a Transit van hired specially for the job.

"We'll look back and laugh at this one day."
"I'm already laughing."
"Too soon."

Whitehaven is the sort of place that could be a cold and shivery spot on a summer's day. At 7am on a January Saturday it's been ramped up a bit from cold and shivery.

Last night, on our way into the town for a refreshing ale, our taxi driver told us some tales of local life. He was particularly keen on the it's-just-health-and-safety-gone-mad type of story, which was interesting, taking into account

his flagrant disregard for seatbelts. He said nothing about local cabbies not being allowed to carry shotguns, which was a surprise to me considering recent history, but there you go. He did tell us about Mad Friday, where the populace of Whitehaven were fighting in the streets by 4.30pm after being in the pubs all day, but the snow came down and they all went home. He has a point. Tottenham, Toxteth, LA, Brixton, all in the summer. You don't hear of the Aberdeen or Anchorage riots, do you?

We're dropped off at a point triangulated to take in the maximum number of unappealing watering holes. There are scary men and hard-faced women in abundance, but bafflingly little in the way of all-weather clothing. A big ginger fellow with a pink face marches past with a belligerent gait and a challenging stare. This doesn't look promising.

"So, this Mad Friday he was talking about, when was that?"
"The day before Christmas Eve, I think."
"Could be Mad Anyday by the looks of things round here."

Opposite: *Traditional wheel-dipping at the start of the C2C in Whitehaven.*

Below: *Trying to warm up by scaling Whinlatter Pass with the smell of woodsmoke rising from Lorton Vale.*

"This could be the most frightening night of my life."

"Look at them. We're going to get our heads kicked in."

This was before we found The Vagabond and its lovely beer and people. What xenophobic idiots we can be. Everywhere has rubbish bits, you just have to find the good bits before you get stabbed.

In theory, you can do the C2C in a day, as it's only about 100 miles, depending which start and finish points you choose. In practice, with the roads being somewhat on the heavy side, most people choose to do it in two. There's also a classic off-road version that people will often spend three hard days on.

With it being the middle of winter and officially The North, we've plumped for the populist two-day road version. That is why I am dipping my tyre into the water at the regenerated harbour, as is traditional, and getting swan poo stuck in the cleats of my road shoes as early-morning pink light starts to colour the clouds above us.

We wind our way out of the curious town on a well-surfaced railway path and head for the hills. We can see a dusting of snow on the heads of the nearest peaks of the western Lakes. Before long we'll meet the day's big challenge, Whinlatter Pass. I'm beginning to warm up.

It's a long, long way up, with some very steep bits, but they are thankfully quite brief, and before long we're dodging icy patches on the way down to Derwentwater and Keswick.

"I saw this thing where two blokes got trapped on Mount Cook for a fortnight."

"They survived?"

"Yeah. They had to make a decision between trying to exercise to keep warm or sitting dead still to conserve heat and energy."

"I'd go for the latter right now."

"Apparently, exercise will give you hypothermia, but keeping still will give you frostbite."

"Is that right?"

"That's what they said. And frostbite will lead to amputation but hypothermia will kill you."

"And they survived, you say?"

"Yeah, but one of them had to have his legs amputated."

Down on Derwentwater, there's a bunch of mallards determined to conserve heat and energy by standing completely still on thick ice.

While we're taking it all in, a car pulls up with an optimistic canoe on the roof and a middle-aged man leaves the warmth of the driver's seat to come down for a look. He is wearing flip-flops. Still trying to process this, I look to my right and watch another middle-aged man try to impress his less-than-impressed partner by jumping up and down 10ft out on the ice. At least we'll have a canoe if he goes through, I suppose.

The light is pinkening once more when we reach the wonderfully unheralded splendour of Castlerigg Stone Circle. These rocks were carefully manoeuvered into place 4,500 years ago, for reasons nobody can yet be certain of. Sitting on a low hill, surrounded by snow-capped mountains in every direction, this remains a special place. A group of rooks, or a parliament of rooks if you're that way inclined, skulk around the far side, eyeing us suspiciously. As Phil snaps away, I stroll up to the outer ring, then come to an abrupt halt.

"Woah! That was weird... I really didn't want to walk into the circle then. Not in a bad way... it just felt... I don't know, a bit rude. A bit wrong."

"Idiot."

"Come on, don't tell me you can't feel any sort of energy about this place? It's amazing."

"Idiot."

"Yeah, but I can't help noticing you were taking pictures over on that side, now you're taking them on this side, yet rather than walk across the middle you walked all the way round the edge."

"Harrumph."

We take some more shots of the darkening sky, then get ready to move off to the beds waiting for us in Penrith.

"I just need to get a few more of the stones... it's annoying, I can't seem to... I want an angle, but... oh sod it, I'm just going to have to go in there, aren't I?"

Previous page:
Derwentwater is under that ice. Skiddaw, the fourth highest mountain in England, is beyond and is easily walked from Keswick.

Below: *Castlerigg Stone Circle at dusk. The Circle is sited in a natural amphitheatre surrounded by high fells, which add to the drama of this amazing spot.*

Penrith, Day Two. I'm not sure I've ever ridden a bike in colder weather, but at least it's not windy. I'm wearing a thermal long-sleeved base layer, a sleeveless base layer, a winter long-sleeved jersey, a soft-shell thermal jacket, windstopper bib tights, winter gloves, a thermal beanie under my helmet, and overshoes. The only bit of me exposed to the elements is the bottom half of my face below my Oakleys. And that bit hurts really, really badly. When we do a short downhill, just as dawn is breaking over the vale between the Pennines and the Lakes, it feels as though my jaw is splintering in the cold. My guess is about minus eight, which I could deal with if I was warmed up, but I'm not. I look across at Phil. He doesn't look thrilled. There's not much talking.

There are grey snow clouds overhead, but the rising sun shoots golden beams beneath them, illuminating the frozen fields and roads in a shimmering beaten-metal glow. From the north, a V of swans appear, not mute swans like we're used to on the Thames, but yellow-billed whoopers or Bewick's, their white

undersides lit up as if they were stage scenery. Perhaps they're nearing the end of their trip from Siberia or Svalbard; if they continue on this line they'll join their families at Slimbridge on the Severn Estuary in a day or two.

In front of us is the wall of the Pennines. The colour of this huge edge of land changes about a third of the way up from grey-green to white. The back roads that form the bulk of the C2C are impassable this morning, so we're on the A686, but we haven't seen a single car yet. The temperature, the ice, and the temptations of a Sunday lie-in have given us glorious solitude in which to enjoy this beautiful morning. For perhaps the first time in my life, I'm approaching a major climb with something more positive than apprehension inside me. Hartside Top is a five-mile drag across barren hillside, today heavy with snow, and 1,600 feet of vertical gain over those miles, but it's a steady gradient all the way, ideal for my size, and the extra effort will warm me through. Plus there's a cafe at the top, though no guarantee it will be open.

Above: *Well below freezing, east of Penrith. The back roads usually used for the C2C are impassable in this weather.*

Opposite: *The Lakes from Hartside Top. This panorama can be viewed from the warmth of "England's highest café."*

The dry stone walls lead us up through a dark wood and on to the open moor, and the vistas to the west begin to open up. Beyond the icy green open fields of Inglewood Forest, the Lakeland Fells rear up in a startling white mantle of snow. High Street above Ullswater is the nearest, 20 miles away, with Blencathra's brooding gable just beyond it. The Munro-bagger's summit of Skiddaw peeks over the northern shoulder of Blencathra, then the flat plains of Wigton and Aspatria (this is actually in Cumbria although ti sounds like Ancient Greece) give way to the Solway Firth and the North Channel. We might see finer views this year but right now that's impossible to imagine.

Phil stops to capture the moment and have a steaming yellow wee, so I plod onwards and upwards and over the snow line in contented solitude. The steady gradient makes climbing a similar exercise to turbo training, which I did a fair bit of in December. Knowing that this trip was coming up, and looking for something to fill the long winter evenings, we set up a Turbo Night on Thursdays at our bike shop on the south

coast. Up to a dozen of us would line up in front of the plasma screen and pedal furiously every time some idiot on the DVD we were watching told us to. The floor needed mopping even on the coldest nights. I dropped a couple of pounds of good autumnal eating and found the rhythm for climbs like this, but I also know there will be plenty more uphill miles to come before we make Tynemouth. It's tempting to think of the C2C as a long haul up from the west coast to a watershed, then an easy swoosh down to the North Sea; needless to say, it isn't.

It's very bleak up here. Signs are coated in a couple of inches of fresh snow. As I approach one, there is a low thump as the snow slips off it in a single blanket, revealing that I am indeed on the C2C, and yes, there's a long way to go.

As I roll up the last few hundred yards of snowy mountain, I can see that the car park at Hartside Top Cafe, normally such a popular spot with motorcyclists, is deserted. A pang of hunger and disappointment shoots through my cold bones, until I see a light in the window, and a welcoming "Open" sign. Result. They open

Above: *Flowers left on a bench, frozen solid. So much for true love.*

Opposite: *A hot stove, warm feet and a full English at the Hartside Café.*

Next page: *Descending through Gilderdale Forest below Cross Fell, the highest point in the Pennines.*

at 10am, and it's five past. I'm straight in there, shoes off in front of the wood burner and a full English on its way. There's a real January feel in the air; it's not just the weather, it's the lack of people and the fact that the proprietors are using a frozen New Year morning to take down the Christmas decorations.

"Motorbike riders always look pretty cool in all their gear, don't they?" muses Phil over a steaming mug of black coffee.

"I suppose," I say, wondering where this is going, seeing as there isn't one in sight.

"But when they take their lids off, they're nearly all 50-plus, with fags hanging out of their mouths. They think they're hard, but frankly, anyone can do this –" he makes a gesture with his right hand, rotating the wrist as though he's revving a throttle, but it could quite embarrassingly be seen in a different way by the public.

"I think quite a lot of them are, yes."

My initial disappointment at not being able to stick to the route-proper in these conditions is tempered by the realisation that long downhills on small roads would be absolutely impossible on 23mm of rubber. Shooting down the larger

road towards Alston past frozen abandoned mine workings, we're glad to see hard, wet tarmac below us instead of the skating rink conditions we've been getting. I'm frozen stiff by the long, chilly descent by the time we hit the buzzing little town, and a little Flandrian cobbled climb up through the middle of the pretty Pennine oasis is just the tonic for shaking my cold-deadened limbs.

There's a brief pause for an energising Clif Bar and a call home.

"How's Jane?"

"Good, pleased to have me out from under her feet for a couple of days I think."

"I imagine her with a big old fashioned two-pieced telephone."

"Wearing a negligée."

"And fluffy mules."

"With huge fake eyebrows. No, I mean eyelashes."

"And a fag."

"In a cigarette holder, like Princess Margaret."

"And a red neckerchief."

"That's too weird. There's a line, you know."

"I see a line; I cross it."

"Oh you maverick."

I like bleak places. Over the next 12 months we'll actively seek them out. I'll be surprised if we pass through anywhere much bleaker than the higher ends of Weardale, though. Can you imagine a better name for an abandoned lead mine in such a remote spot as Killhope? Well put, Mr Placenamegiver.

A couple more long warming drags and we're dropping into Consett. Disappointingly, our route doesn't take us along Medomsley Road, but you'll be relieved to hear that this doesn't stop us from saying "Medomsley Road, Consett," every few yards in faux Victorian voices in celebration of the old Phileas Fogg tortilla chips adverts. This is one of our all-time favourite advert things to say, but is naturally beaten into a distant runner-up by the builder in the van singing "Fried Onion Rings" to the tune of Que Sera Sera in honour of what he will choose to accompany his Bird's Eye Steakhouse Grill. We, on the other hand, always hope "It's chips, it's chips."

The architecture in these parts is either grim or Last-of-the-Summer-Wine solid-but-pretty depending on your mood or the weather. I am particularly amused at the optimist who has a string of washing out in the garden.

"That'll be frozen as stiff as a board now."
"Maybe they put it out in August and they're just waiting for it to dry."

My legs are hurting now. My bum hurts too. My fingers are wet (wrong gloves) and stinging. I don't even want to talk about my feet, and I'm sure you don't either. Fortunately, it's in Consett that we pick up the rather lovely railway path that follows the Derwent Valley all the way down into Newcastle.

Right: *Newcastle's many Tyne crossings were either built high enough to let ships pass below, or moveable to let them through.*

We've picked Tynemouth as our finishing point rather than the alternative of Sunderland, largely for the ride along the Tyne under all the beautiful high bridges of Newcastle, but the unexpected delights of this easy traffic-free stretch do just as much to convince us that we'd made a good choice. The C2C is very good on lovely quiet lanes, it must be said, even if we've

National Cycle Network

C2C FINISH

START

Hadrian's Cycleway

72

Reivers

10

Coast & Castles

1

had to miss a lot of them out thanks to the snow and ice higher up.

Those bridges sure are cool. There's something special about Newcastle: it's a proper city. The way the big buildings are drawn from so many different eras and styles, yet are wedged in tight to each other gives it a cosmopolitan feel even before you've begun to experience the warmth of the locals. People like living here, so there is a lot less of the breast-beating, misplaced pride that seems to form the backdrop for so many of Britain's provincial cities. The way the football stadium sits proudly over the town, the way the club genuinely represents the place and its people in a way that's usually only found in much smaller centres of population seems to have a lot to do with it, too.

Out the other side of town, you can smell the North Sea on the air as the Tyne widens.

It's starting to get dark with the short winter afternoon drawing in, but we remembered the lights for once. Along with some other friends, Phil and I got caught out in a rather major way on the South Downs a couple of years ago; untold punctures meant we ran out of spare tubes and the extra time spent fixing holes left us riding down the A29 in the pitch black. I wouldn't recommend it.

We find Mark waiting for us with the van in Tynemouth. He's been struggling to find diesel after mistakenly following signs for the Metro believing them to be leading him to Morrisons. "It's the same design 'M!'"

As is traditional, we bump down the cliff to the beach to dip our tyres into the North Sea to symbolically complete the trip and are rewarded by a rising yellow moon. The bikes will feel rough with sand tomorrow, but I don't care; my legs will feel much the same.

Below: *The Tyne widens majestically into the North Sea, the lights of South Shields illuminating the south bank.*

February

South Downs Way

I am having an artistic flounce.

"But I can't possibly write at home. I must go to Marwood's immediately."

"Why can't you write at home?"

"I don't have a desk. I don't even have a table."

"Can't you write in the big chair?"

"Yes, I can write in the big chair, as long as you can finance a spinal replacement tomorrow."

"That thing you write on is actually called a laptop, you know."

"Yes, it is called a laptop. However that pad you use to fiddle with Photoshop all day is called a tablet. There's as much chance of me bending double and balancing this on my knees so I can get writing as there is of you dissolving two of those in a glass of water."

"What's so good about Marwood's anyway?"

"They have very good coffee and relatively flat tables."

"Last time you went there, you came back so wired you had eyes like Charlie Sheen and were ordering Shriekback CDs on Amazon until four in the morning."

"Yes, but that's because they have a sign behind the counter showing a scary sort of dominatrix lady with a speech bubble saying, 'Hey! You with the laptop! Buy some more coffee!' Do you know what their WiFi password is? 'buymorecoffee.'"

"That's quite funny."

"Yeah, it is quite funny."

"So why do you really go there?"

"Well, the coffee really is really nice. And the tables really are quite flat. And girls go there."

"Ahhh, now I see.

Left: *Early morning on Truleigh Hill. The coastal plain on the south side of the South Downs ridge is invariably warmer than the Wealden side.*

It would be fair to say that it's a bit parky in Winchester at six in the morning in February. It's also pretty dark. Our aim is to get rolling on the South Downs Way and get to the top of the first hill before the sun comes up.

"Alfred the Great was crowned in Winchester, you know."

"The one that burnt the cakes?"

"That is the single most boring and predictable thing that you can say about Alfred the Great. The man personally responsible for saving England. The only king we've ever had who is known as 'The Great'. He burnt some cakes. That's as boring as playing Monopoly and saying, 'Imagine if this was real money.'"

"Alright, keep your thinning hair on. I thought the Saxon kings were crowned in Kingston?"

"Ah, yeah, but when Alfred got the call, Kingston was full of Vikings. They were at war, they had to do it on the hoof."

"Yeah, but Kingston, Kings' Town, isn't it?"

"You'd think, wouldn't you? But apparently, in the Domesday Book, which incidentally was put together here in Winchester, Kingston is called Chingestone, so it's just a coincidence."

"Seems to me you're the boring one. So boring I can scarcely believe my bored ears."

The sun is threatening the eastern horizon as we skip over the frosty fields leading up to the improbably named Cheesefoot Head. The ground is good and hard under the rubber, the air crispy, the sky clear. It's a special morning. Cheesefoot Head sits above a fantastically round natural amphitheatre in the lap of the Downs.

"This is where Eisenhower addressed the troops before D-Day."

"On B- or C-Day probably, then."

"And where they used to have the Homelands

Festival. So Kraftwerk must have been on here. I think."

"Enough with the facts for God's sake. It's only seven o'clock in the morning."

"Sorry."

I phoned my ex the night before we set out.

"So... err... happy birthday."

"Thank you."

"Erm... bit tricky this one, but I bought you a present before we broke up. Do you still want it?"

"That's nice of you, what is it?"

"Well, it's a present, isn't it? You're meant to open it and find out. So do you want it or not?"

"Sure, as long as you're happy with that."

"Well, no I'm not happy with it at all. I'm not **** happy full stop."

"Why are you swearing?"

"Because that's what I do now! I swear! ****! ****! See?"

"Yeah. Bye, thanks for ringing."

Such unresolved issues may explain why I'm so irritating today. I mean, more irritating than usual, you know what I mean.

Phil – Believe me, this exchange only scratches the surface of what he was like. I just switched off, to be honest.

The South Downs Way is genuinely beautiful. It has a kind of neatness about it, as the South Downs themselves are an obvious feature in Hampshire and even more so in Sussex, where a ridge route along the lip of the low hills is clear for the whole length of the range. In fact, it always comes as a surprise when you reach a signpost and your direction is to the left or right rather than straight ahead. Navigation is simple and the point of the journey is always apparent, especially when tackled from west to east like this: stay on the hills until you reach the sea and can go no further.

At about 100 miles, It's a ride that is doable in a day, and if we had scheduled this particular trip for later in the year, the long evenings and hard chalky paths may well have tempted us into doing it in one hit. There is even an elite club for those who've done the whole thing there and back in under 24 hours. A friend of ours, Leitchy, held the record for a couple of years: Winchester to Eastbourne to Winchester in a shade over 18 hours. I know! However, there are couple of pitfalls lying in wait for the unwary.

Firstly, for all the talk of ridge riding, there are a lot of hills to ride up. A lot of hills. Even the lightning fast, rutted, channelled, chalky descents take it out of you, as they hammer your arms into submission. This is a ridge with a thousand interruptions.

Secondly, the soil, baked hard in periods of dry weather, turns into a skating rink with a spattering of rain, a spread of Copydex in winter mildness, and a mud wrestling pit after a soaking. Better riders than us (that'll be most people) have hurled their bikes into ancient hedgerows in disgust at their lack of progress when all appears simple.

There is also something perfect about these hills on a crisp, winter day. The close cropped grass, blue, blue skies and hazy views allied to a sparkling English Channel down to your right occasionally all combine to make these paths a popular destination on frosty weekends. So we plumped for a two-day trip in February, breaking the trip in the rarified atmosphere of Arundel, roughly halfway between Winchester and Eastbourne. We kept a close eye on the weather, and ended up getting it just about bob on, as Phil would say.

Right: *In February, the weak winter sun will often fail to find the strength to burn off frost for days on end.*

"Bob on. Where does that come from?"

"What do you mean?"

"I mean you're the only person I've ever heard say something is 'bob on.' Bob's yer uncle, bob-a-job. Bang on. Spot on. I've heard all of them."

"It's actually in common usage. Bob on. Everybody says it."

"No they don't."

"Yes they do."

"Let's ask the next person we see."

Fortunately we don't see anybody for a long, long time, and by then we've forgotten all about it. The burbling Meon and its green watercress beds take our attention.

They've been hedge-cutting, and we get an early puncture. We're both well aware of the mistake we made down this way a couple of years back when we failed to re-inflate tyres to the required pressure after a flat.

You need about 40psi in your off-road tyres up here if you weigh what I weigh. Otherwise, the first one of those mental descents will see you crunch your front wheel into a flinty rut, squeeze the tyre against the rim, pinch the tube and leave you back at square one.

Phil – I must admit to finding the South Downs tricky to photograph. It's unquestionably beautiful, but the glorious long views don't really lend themselves to pictures as they're often without a focal point. In the end, though it may sound blasé, when you've seen one huge, hazy panorama from a grassy Sussex hilltop, you've seen them all.

I didn't feel I was doing the overall feel of the route justice: you get a sort of contentment and enjoyment that's hard to match elsewhere. I ended up taking a lot more pictures of the two of us and what we were doing than I normally would.

By the time we swing down the Arun Valley to finish our day, my arms feel like they've been beaten by a Taleban inquisitor. I won't go into what my backside feels like.

There's a pub in Arundel with my name on it. In fact, a few pubs. Best not get too drunk though, long way tomorrow... I said, best not get too drunk... I said... oh, never mind.

On another topic, I love sunglasses. I specifically love Oakleys. Through judicious collecting and profligate curatorship, I have amassed and subsequently lost a collection of 30 or more pairs over the years. At the moment, I am mostly wearing some Batwolfs with interchangeable icons. If you have to ask, I couldn't possibly make you understand, that's just the way it is. I wear them all day and all night, largely perched on my head. This is where Oakleys always win out over rival brands: they stick to your head.

"Isn't it a bit dark for sunglasses?"

"Yes. That is why they are –" (gesticulating in the air above my head like a patronising children's television presenter) "on my head, and not –" (similar hand movement in front of my face) "over my eyes."

"Yes, but it's been dark for hours and we're just going out. Why would you put them on? Do you think the sun might suddenly and unexpectedly rise? Or do you suspect you might need to mask a black eye before you come home?"

"No. It is because I am a rock star and chicks dig me."

It's really because I am going for one of the classic cover-up methods of distracting attention away from male pattern baldness. Now, anybody who has seen a photograph of Phil's dad in early middle age, or indeed, seen the boy himself beginning to thin out in his mid-twenties, could have predicted he would have been deflecting searchlight beams back into the eyes of helicopter pilots whil still a young man. These facts and Phil's stoic disposition means that he bears his bareness lightly. I, however, with the asset of two grandfathers carrying full shocks of hair into retirement, was singularly unprepared for the need to wear a hat to avoid cranial sunburn in my 30s. Because I, as we have ascertained, am a rock star and chicks dig me, I have a certain reputation that my public demands of me, and for that I need to use one of the classic cover-up methods.

Phil – Quick translation for those reading in the language of the non-self-obsessed: "Because I am a rock star and chicks dig me, I have a certain reputation that my public demands of me," means "I am a prat."

As everybody knows, the number one classic cover-up is the hat. I have lots of hats. Some of them are even good hats. The Oakley classic cover-up is my personal favourite method, though. The classic cover-up of choice for the new money generation is clearly the Rooney Plug, or its smart variation, the Barlow Weave. Remember when Gary Barlow was receding? It's grown back! Still, all better than the least convincing classic cover-up of all time – the Mark Knopfler headband. What was all that about?

We start in the dark again. I'll admit to enjoying this. It's exciting, but not as scary as you might think. For our work Christmas party a couple of years ago we went night mountain biking, ending up at a pub. I hope I don't sound like too much of a sad case when I tell you that it was the best Christmas do I've ever been on.

It's dead, dead cold, and a big, warming climb to get back on the ridge from Amberley is actually quite welcome.

Then we revisit a conversation that's been ticking away for a few weeks.

"Jane doesn't like it."

"Girls don't like the idea of it, but they quite like it when you actually do it."

"Really?"

"Well, once they get over the shock, you know."

"Do you tell her that you're going to do it beforehand, or just dive straight in?"

"Just go for it. What's the worst thing that can happen?"

This is the age-old cyclist's dilemma and every year, I tell myself this: you're old. You're a bit fat. You were never any good at cycling when you were young and slim either. Why, in heaven's name, would you shave your legs? And then, the first warm ride of spring, the shorts come out for the first time, you're out in the lanes, feeling the sun on your face, feeling great to be alive, until you look down... ugh! Lycra plus hairy legs! No! This is a dilemma that Phil is facing for the first time, and not with the full support of his family, it would seem.

The first few miles are spent diving into thick mist patches then back into bright white sunshine. As the cloud rises around us on Devil's Dyke, a voice can be heard plaintively repeating the same word, though we can't make it out exactly. It could be Fenton. I like to think so, as the mist parts to show us a dog-walking diorama of wagging tales, wellington boots and one errant terrier determined to plough his own lonely furrow and ignore the rising calls for his return. (If you don't know who Fenton is, YouTube him for a real treat.)

"What is Devil's Dyke exactly?"

"A dyke is a man-made ditch I think. So I thought it was the old hill-fort."

"Nothing to do with Brighton girls then?"

"Don't think so. Usually, when something is the Devil's, it means bigger than normal, so only

the Devil could have made it'. Like the Devil's Causeway and the Devil's Staircase. So I suppose it could just be this valley is like a massive ditch."

"That makes sense. Let's go."

At Lewes, we descend in search of sustenance. We find it in abundance, as a phalanx of yummy mummies shoulder each other around the farmer's market. Since we're well ahead of our very comfortably arranged schedule, we have time to rub their shoulders for them if they want, but nobody asks. Instead, we settle for a rather delicious brunch at a well-appointed cafe and enjoy a bit of pre-spring sunshine. I try to persuade Phil to buy some of the overpriced tat on offer, but he's having none of it. Pink French lemonade is apparently not on today's menu. Nice place, Lewes, but god, does it know it.

Not far from Lewes, as we clamber to the top of yet another lung buster, is Firle Beacon. In the sky are 30 or so paragliders. It's a beautiful sight, and it strikes me that their number outweighs the amount of bike-borne enthusiasts that we've come across over the last two days. A lasting memory for me will be watching a thermal-riding buzzard weave in and out of the bright canopies with absolute indifference.

"My Nan and Grandad came to Alfriston on their honeymoon. By bus, I think. Do you think it's named after Alfred the Great?"

"I'm not actually listening, so save your breath, you're so boring."

In Alfriston, there is a splendid shop that sells most things, and all the things it sells are good. I buy a pastie, Phil buys a scone.

Left: *Sharing the sky over Firle Beacon. With a northerly breeze, this is southern England's favourite paragliding venue.*

"One scone, please," says the lady on the till to her tabard-wearing colleague working the fresh stuff cabinet. She says it to rhyme with "cone".

"It's scone," says Phil, rhyming it with 'on'. "Because when you eat it, it's gone."

The lady doesn't laugh. She doesn't even smile. She looks at Phil as if she thinks he might be real trouble, but if he were to make a move, she would be sure to get her retaliation in first.

Outside, there is a rumbling noise as if the truck out of Duel is approaching with a wrecked engine and a flat tyre. It's actually a lowered 'R' reg Subaru Impreza with an air intake on the roof. Country ways. When it pulls up, a girl gets out wearing painted-on leggings, something that looks like a cross between a boob-tube and a fisherman's sweater, and so much make-up it's amazing she can hold her head up. She looks like she wants to maul the next person she sees. She is also wearing the most ludicrous pair of studded six-inch high mules known to man. I look around, but see no film crew tracking her movements.

At this point, I have a revelation. I am now old. I know this, because upon taking all this in, I look at the shoes and the first thought that comes into my mind is: "How can she drive safely with those on?"

After Alfriston, we make a small change to the route. The South Downs Way has two routes from here, one for riders of bikes and horses that carries on eastwards along the ridge, then drops into Eastbourne. Walkers follow the Cuckmere Valley down to the white cliffs known as the Seven Sisters, then over Beachy Head and down to the finish where it meets the bridleway version. Years ago, when I was first an intrepid biker, you could ride either route, but gradual erosion of the cliffs put a stop to that, and now you have to go the other way if you're in the saddle.

Now, we happen to know that there is a great route for bikers that goes up the humungous Windover Hill out of Alfriston, then leaves the Way to duck south and into the marvellous tree-lined singletrack of Friston Forest. After that, you can take one of the best cycling roads in the South East up over Beachy Head, thus enjoying the same views as the walkers, but without eroding the cliffs. Everybody's happy. So that's what we do.

The frost has either dissipated by this time in the afternoon, or was never present in the forest thanks to the tree canopy. As a result, the top layer of soil is sketchier than Rolf Harris's notebook, and it's a chore just to keep a straight line. The uphills are most frustrating, as expressions of raw power (that's me all over) just result in a wheelspin and a foot down. And once you've put that foot down, it's really hard to get rolling again for the same reason. Phil seems to be better at this than me. Sweary John makes a reappearance. Sorry to anyone who may have been sharing the forest with us on that afternoon. I've got pills for it now.

Right: Phil tackles the gradient through the beech woods. Downland climbing is made more difficult by slippery chalk and roots.

Once, when I was ill in bed, I complained to my girlfriend, "What the hell is that noise?"

"What noise?"

"That rhythmic grunting noise. Is it them upstairs? Have they started having sex again?"

"At their age?"

"Well what is it then?"

"It's you. Every time you breathe out, you do a little groan. Like you've just discovered you've trod in a turd. Urgh. Urgh. Urgh. All frickin' night." She really did used to say "frickin'".

Halfway up the final climb to Beachy Head, I realise I am making that noise again. I can't blame it on influenza or rampant geriatric neighbours. This was meant to be the easiest ride of the year; the one that you can do in a day but we're doing in two, the one that some people ride there and back in one go. And here I am, shattered. Stuck to the ground. Going backwards. All that stuff. Finally, FINALLY,

we're over the top, past suicide corner. I would have, but I was too tired. The glittering lights of Eastbourne on a clear, accelerated February evening are waiting for us far below: from here, we can make it to the end without even turning the pedals again. So I won't.

"Wow! Look at that! It's like the Riviera!"

"Have you ever been to the Riviera?"

"No."

"You say it looks like the Riviera, but you've never been there?"

"I've never been to the South Pole, but I know what it looks like."

"You've never been to Nice, though?"

"No, but I've eaten the biscuits."

"Biscuits?"

"Yeah, Nice biscuits."

"What are they like?"

"Nice."

Left: *Beachy Head, where the South Downs chop away sharply into the English Channel.*

March

Tour of Flanders

This is it. The best weekend of the year. Right here, right now.

The Tour of Flanders is like FA Cup Final day in Belgium. Or, more accurately, like FA Cup Final day was when we were kids. The whole Flemish nation lines the roads to watch their heroes at close quarters. Uniquely in world sport, Joe Public can get on his bike to ride the route the day before. If it were indeed the FA Cup Final, there would be 20,000 of us having a kick-about at Wembley on the Friday before the game.

Back rumbling through Flemish fields in spring again, the thing that you recognise first isn't the thing you might expect. You would think that the cobbles that ruptured your spleen last year would ring a bell. You might think that the sound of a kindly local shouting "Op, op, op!" in your ear as you try to maintain forward momentum up another backbreaking cart track would be familiar. You might even remember the disconnection of your cleats slipping on the setts as you try to walk your bike up that same hill when it all gets too much. But no. The thing that immediately, unquestionably plonks you right back in Flanders is the smell.

Occasionally, it's the twenty-first century choke of chemical fertiliser, but, for the vast majority of the time, it's the timeless cheesy rotten stench of chicken poo, spread across the fields to promote the green shoots that are sprouting from the plough-churned grey soil. It probably doesn't smell like this in summer, autumn or winter, but I wouldn't know: who on earth wants to be anywhere but here at this time of year? Obversely, why would you ever come here at any other time? This is the Ronde van Vlaanderen.

Left: Grinding up the Paterberg, one of the many steep cobbled climbs that litter the second half of the Tour of Flanders.

How could you be a cycling fan and not want to "do" the Tour of Flanders? Everything about this trip is epic: a weekend in one of the world's most captivating cities, joining 20,000 people to ride the most amazing sportive in world cycling, then watching the best race of the year tackle the same roads you so proudly conquered the day before.

This is where *12 Months in the Saddle* all started for us. Ironically, it was 12 months ago. My fourth Flanders, Phlash's second. We were covering the weekend for cycling magazine readers in Australia dreaming of Old World bike races. We had collapsed at the top of the Keppelmuur, knowing there were just ten more miles separating us from a cold beer in Ninove.

"You know what we should do?"
"Wassat, then?"
"Keep writing about these. I'll take pictures. It's got to be better than photographing

Christmas Hampers in February."
"You've had worse ideas."

Most of this book is a stumble in the dark, as you will no doubt have recognised by now. But this is one trip we know all about. So if you ignore everything else we come out with, listen to us on this one and do as you're told, OK? Get to Belgium on Friday, ride the event on Saturday, watch the pro race on Sunday, get home in time for last orders on Sunday night.

Step one: go to Bruges. Ghent is cool, Oudernaarde is cycling central, but Bruges, as Ralph Fiennes swears in the film, is like a fairy tale. Rock up to your dirt cheap hostel right in the centre of the fourteenth-century canal-ringed medieval Brothers Grimm film set on the Friday morning, and you'll have all day to buy chocolate, beer and lace. OK, forget the lace, get some frites to go with your chocolate and beer instead. Crucially, get a car. You're

Above: *Many of the roads used by the Tour of Flanders are too small to appear on my map.*

going to need it to make the most of your stay. As a Johnny Foreigner, you're probably going to have to drive the hour or so down to the Race HQ in Oudenaarde to sign on and pick up your number for the ride tomorrow.

A few months ago, munching your Christmas dinner, thinking of what your big target was going to be for this year, you already made the big decision about which of the three available distances you were going to do. You have clearly not come all this way to just do the 75km ride, so we can write that off. The tricky choice is whether you go the whole 260km hog, or the popular 140 – 170km (it varies) version? While you might think that the full distance is a prerequisite for this trip, there are a number of things counting against it. Firstly, the main plan of the race organisers is to bore the riders to death over the initial 100km: it's all on long, straight roads traversing the dullest territory to be found in Europe. You will have nothing but a crosswind to entertain you. Secondly, it presents something of a logistical nightmare, as the start in Bruges is an hour's buzz up the motorway from the finish in Oudenaarde. Your 260km day could be 400km if you're not careful. They lay on a shuttle, but you'll have to leave at 5am.

John and Phil say: get up at 7am. Drive down to Oudenaarde. Park up on one of the handy grim industrial estates. You have now got in the region of 160km in front of you once you have ridden the last bit of the journey to the HQ, completed the Ronde, and ridden back through the town to your car after the finish on the other side of town.

Below: *Many of the chocolate shops in Bruges allow you to watch the manufacturing process of the coveted narcotic.*

Next page: *Cycling and more chocolate, Bruges-style.*

Above: John's legs. NB: Not really John's legs.

"The thing about Belgium is you're never really anywhere, but you're never in the middle of nowhere. You could take a cricket ball, throw it from house to house and never have it fall short of somebody's property."

"I never thought I'd hear myself say this: I know exactly what you mean."

"It's like you're forever on the outskirts of somewhere. And what about the houses? They're unbelievable."

"They're neater than a James Bond villain's underground lair. Especially if it was designed by Fisher-Price."

"Do you think it's because they all got destroyed during the war, or wars, and had to start again from scratch?"

"Hmm. Maybe. But Coventry or Portsmouth don't look like that, do they?"

"Like they model themselves on Munchkinland? No."

It's not until you get south of the River Schelde to where the low hills of the Flemish Ardennes crouch that there is anything to look at in the slightest. But fear not, traveller, for that is where we are headed. Even these hills aren't much to look at, to be honest. Vaguely reminiscent of the North Downs in Surrey and Kent, they aren't as high as Box Hill or Leith Hill. However, they have shaped the character of the Ronde van Vlaanderen since it began in 1913. Because what they lack in height, they

make up for in difficulty. In spades. They're really, really steep. And they're cobbled. There are 16 climbs for us to go up in 2012. Not all cobbled, but all horrible.

There is an air of controversy about this year's event, stemming from the decision to move the finish from Meerbeke on the outskirts of Ninove up to Oudenaarde. The real issue here is Meerbeke, a particularly unloved corner of an unloved land. In fact, this race used to start in a similar location: my first memories of Flanders involved a roll-out in the God-forsaken hole of St Niklaas. Heaven forbid you ever have to spend Christmas there. The shift to Bruges has been universally applauded and rightly so. Moving the finish to Oudenaarde,

home to the Flanders Cycling Museum and untold cobble-eating lycra-abusing overweight cyclists, has some precedent. It's also closer to hills like the Kwaremont, Paterberg, Kruisberg, Berendries, Molenberg, Taaienberg and Valkenberg, and the fabulous Koppenberg is right above the town.

But, and it's a big but, the Belgian cycling public were outraged when they realised that moving the finish would mean sacrificing the holy finishing run-in of Tenbosse, Muur and Bosberg. I for one was a little bit sad that we wouldn't be watching the race being decided on the Muur in Geraardsbergen like it has been many times over the years. But I sure as hell wouldn't miss riding up the thing.

Now is the time to enjoy the full spectrum of fashions on view: yellow shorts on wide arses, jerseys advertising the meats available in local *slagerijs*, grey woolly socks. One group of clubmates are sponsored by a plumbing company that revels in the uncompromising name of Sani-Dump. Bikes branded with improbable English family names like Ridley, Thomson or Stevens. These people share something in common with Lance Armstrong: it really isn't about the bike. It's about how you ride it. To a man, or, much less likely at this event, to a woman, they all know what they're doing. You'll have to look hard to see someone with their saddle five centimetres too low turning 53 x 13 at 15mph. They don't pedal three strokes then freewheel for 50yd. And they very, very rarely stand up on the pedals. If you do see a girl, she's more than likely foreign, and if she's foreign, she's more than likely British. The usually bike-clogged weekend roads of England must be empty today, because it feels like they're all here, either proudly sporting the excruciating jerseys of their crushingly provincial bike clubs or Rapha'd up to the max.

Cruising along on the unlovely concrete rural roads, it's a good idea to get into a group. When you catch one, it's tempting to overtake them, but it's a lot more sensible to get on somebody's wheel and let them take care of the crosswinds for a while. Trust me, there will be a crosswind. Here comes your first real problem. It's the Taaienberg, only a little climb, but 10 percent on cobbles is a bit of a shock. If you stand on the pedals, your tyres slip on the shiny surface. If you sit down, you run the risk of slowing down so much that you lose all momentum.

Left: *Lunch on the Oude Kwaremont. People get here early to stake out the best spots.*

Momentum is the key. Lose it, and you're lost. The Eikenberg is much the same, and the narrow first corner of the tiny Molenberg is an absolute horror.

Give a look of thanks up to the pale grey heavens that this isn't 2008. By now, you would be soaked to the bone, blasted by a westerly typhoon and chilled to well below your comfort zone. Many of those reaching this point turned and headed back up the main road, thinking only of the shelter of their cars, parked 30km

Below: The Koppenberg is the steepest of all the climbs, maxing out at 22 percent.

away on a dual carriageway outside Ninove. They weren't stupid.

Next up is a little hill that goes by the name of the Koppenberg in these parts. In the 1980s, faltering on the 22 percent section whilst leading, the Jesper Skibby was scandalously knocked off his bike by the race referee's following car. Fearing that the bunch would soon envelop them, the driver ploughed on, driving over Skibby's bike while the Dane was still clipped into his pedals and screaming in

outrage. As a result, the road was left out of the route for the rest of the century. But you'll be delighted to hear it's back. But it's OK. You're OK. You've beaten a couple of bullying hills. You can do this.

Just swing around this dead corner at walking pace, notice the little plaque by the cottages that says Koppenbergstraat, and – holy hamstrings. Look at that. In front of you is a road that looks like a climbing wall. It's nearly vertical and there are hundreds of people in brightly coloured clothing hanging on to it to avoid plummeting to a crunching doom. If I were you, I'd get off now.

But you don't, do you? You're going to make it up the Koppenberg, you're going to beat the two-metre wide 22 percent sod, with its half a mile of stupid archaic squared-off stones... when oh when is tarmac going to arrive in this country? But you can't beat it, because even if you had the legs, somebody in front of you has fallen off, and everybody is stopping. You'll never know. Now is the moment that you're glad you sneakily swapped your road shoes for SPDs. The mahogany-legged poseurs around you may ride their bikes quicker than you, but you can sure as hell kick their arses in a walking race.

The view across the north as you begin to descend is stunning. Why do these people go so slowly downhill? Surely this is what bike riding is all about? Just let it go, a sweeping right hander, stay off the brakes, a tighter left hander, actually, quite a lot tighter, more like 90 degrees and JESUS CHRIST you're a nanosecond from going headfirst into the biggest pile of manure in Belgium. If your legs were shaking from the cobbles, everything else is shaking now from the shock of narrowly avoiding a pungent death.

Right: *Short, but steep: the Molenberg's first ramps can catch out the unwary.*

Gulp in a few more lungfuls of the foul-smelling air as you cross the freshly-spread fields. Find yourself next to a group of Americans mocking each other, one of whom seems to be riding a Serotta that bolts together in the middle so he can get it in a suitcase: in my local bike shop, they'd call that broken. "Heeeyyy, how was that for ya, Cletus?" "It was aaahhhsum, dude."

It's a daze now. Hills come and go. Feedstations pass. You've lost all sense of direction. A long stretch of cobbles you hoped you'd avoided returns to shake the hair out of your head. Your wedding ring shot off somewhere and you've lost both your bottles. You do what you've been told, putting it in a bigger gear, taking more weight on your feet, trying not to grip the bars too tightly, but it's really not helping. Then you remind yourself that it's OK, because this year you won't be going up the Muur.

The Muur. The Keppelmuur. The Muur de Grammont. You have to be a real bitch of a climb to have this many names. You already know the Muur is bad, because it's the only road you've ever seen that looks steep on TV. What will you be missing?

You've just ridden the hardest four hours of your life. You're screwed. Nailed to the road. Can you just walk up it in contemplative solitude? No, afraid not, because it's packed with people shouting at you, encouraging you, pushing the people who've stopped and want to get going again. You CANNOT stop, no matter how steep it is. When you finally come round the last corner, gasping for breath like a goldfish on the kitchen floor, quads burning, eyes watering, ears bleeding, it's out of the dark tunnel and trees and into the sunshine bathing the domed chapel in front of you, and you are redeemed my son. Miss it? Like I miss nits. Like I miss Kim Jong-Il. Like I miss exams. Of course, if you're really keen, you could ride down to Geraardsbergen after you've finished and ride up. Be my guest. Knock yourself out.

Instead, you're bound for the Oude Kwaremont. The Kwaremont has a long draggy start on a little lane before the cobbles kick in, and they are seriously knackered cobbles, trashed by hundreds of years of farmers' boots, horses' hooves and cyclists' broken wheels. You know you're in this deep now, and you're probably wondering if it's all been a big mistake. You can't even rest over the top, as the cobbles drag on vaguely upwards for another klick, before you plunge down back into the same valley and swing a sudden right... oh no, here we go again, you haven't even got your breath back and you're on the Paterberg. This one is 20 percent, so you try and get into the little concrete drainage channel at the side of the setts but you get slower, and slower and slower, until the guy in front of you gives up and clicks out. Are you moving quick enough to jump out round him? If you don't, you'll be seriously annoyed, because it's only another 30 seconds of anaerobic torture to the top.

Not far now. You're glad you upgraded to carbon. OK, nothing's going to make those cobbles comfy, unless you could swap to an 8in travel downhill mtb for those bits, but these awful backside-numbing slabs of concrete that pass for roads sure tell you a few things about your body when they talk via the medium of aluminium. You're glad you put those 25c tyres on, because you've seen the number of people slipping on the shiny stones, and you've seen that guy in the white legwarmers fixing at least three punctures, even though he clearly rides three times as fast as you. Now you're dreaming about beer. It's just a couple of kilometres away. And tonight, you're going to destroy a steak the size of a head, rare to the point of refrigerated, blood oozing out all over your frites, chewing each mouthful like it's your rival's flesh. And you're going to love it.

Right: *You are never far from the smell of smoked meat gently sizzling at the Tour of Flanders*

Opposite: No trip to Flanders would be complete without sampling the correct local method of refuelling.

Below: Space is at a premium on the Oude Kwaremont. Claim the best viewing spot before dashing up to the giant screen for the denouement.

This road is long and straight and has barriers along each side. A banner tells us there are 5km to go. Then 2km. Then just 1,000m to the line. Four lads wearing Perth Cycling Club jerseys pick up the pace, so I switch on to the back of their line, wondering if they're from Scotland or Western Australia. There's no time to find out, because a Belgian guy has opened up the sprint. It's surely too far out, but Phlash (that's Phil) is tight to my wheel and I don't want to give him a sniff of the line so I take the wheel and follow the Belgian past the Perthians. Tragically, as his nose hits the wind, he dies a slow death,

squeezing me into slower moving traffic on the right as Phlash shoots by on the left with 200m to go. Furious, I begin my sprint all over again, anger giving me just enough oomph to pop past him right on the line.

"I had to wait for you up every hill. And then you go and do that. Cheek."

"There was no finish line on the hills."

"Oh, and you'd have beaten me up them if there was?"

"You know what the golfers say: drive for show, putt for dough."

Some of the Belgian beers have three versions. Chimay, for instance, comes in Chimay, Chimay Double, or Chimay Triple. It is all to do with the brewing process, but I like to think that where they use water as the key component in Chimay, with Chimay Double they start with Chimay. And for Chimay Triple, they start with Chimay Double. That's why they taste like medicine and make you go mental.

When you're standing on the Oude Kwaremont on Sunday afternoon, you will need the Triple to help you forget about how your backside feels. Because this morning, when you strolled through the crowd leaning on the barriers shouting for Tom Boonen and Fabian Cancellara as they made their way to the sign on, your backside, well let's just say, it didn't feel too good. In fact, your rear end probably looks much like that pavé of ribeye you butchered last night. Hang on... pavé? Doesn't that mean cobble?

The Kwaremont is the spot to be on Sunday. This year, to combat the loss of the Muur, the organisers are sending the pros up it three times. Before that, the women's World Cup event will come past too. With everybody gunning to be in the first 20 riders when it hits the bottom, nobody wants to get caught behind the crashes that inevitably stack up when you wedge hundreds of speeding riders into a cobbled uphill funnel. When you've screamed in their ears and pushed the fallers back on their way, you can follow them up to the top, drink Triple, eat spicy hotdogs, and watch the last 80km on the big screen in the square by the church.

If you're lucky enough to time your visit to coincide with a Flandrian winning his third Tour of Flanders, this will be the best moment of the entire weekend. And it has been a truly excellent weekend.

Opposite: *Rubbing shoulders with the stars: Fabian Cancellara at the start in Bruges.*

Above: *The square at the top of the Oude Kwaremont stays busy for hours after the race has passed.*

Next page: *Two former world champions and Flanders winners: Alessandro Ballan leads Tom Boonen on the Oude Kwaremont.*

April

Paris-Roubaix

It was the early 90s, and it was the second Sunday in April. I had been following the arcane world of cycling for a few years, greedily lapping up Channel 4's coverage of the Tour de France until I was an undoubted expert in what cyclists do in July. Other races remained a foreign land, illuminated occasionally by stunning images of hardship in magazines published months after the events they were describing had taken place. Shots of battered, muddied and bloodied bike riders taken during races seemingly run in the dark in grim northern European locations, where the entire landscape appeared to be constructed out of bricks, dirt and cobbles.

I had heard rumours that a friend had satellite television. This was a weird new invention that enabled you to watch documentaries about Hitler, sharks and the Titanic, live football matches, and, if you were a lad, films of the more biologically instructive kind after your parents had gone to bed. It also had bike racing on, via the almost impossibly exotic Eurosport channel. It showed every sport on the planet as long as it involved wheels or skiing and had adverts in German. The cycling coverage was delivered by a man who had quite clearly lost his grip on reality some time in between the discovery of the Americas and the US withdrawal from Vietnam. His ill-informed but enthusiastic ramblings were a fantastic antidote to the near-omnipresent hospital radio DJ voices of all the other Eurosport commentators, who Smashie-and-Nicie'd their way through 24/7 biathlon, Moto GPs and monster truck racing.

On this day I had infiltrated the lounge of this distant friend using subterfuge and deception with the sole aim of watching the world's most famous one-day bike race, Paris-Roubaix.

Left: *Near Troisvilles. This is where the ride begins to get interesting.*

No sooner had the motorcycling gone off air, an hour later than scheduled, than we were parachuted into a chaotic chariot race of scarcely fathomable lunacy, grown men attempting to propel racing bikes through oceans of mud and stones more suitable to the pages of *Birdsong* than modern sport. As I sat open mouthed at the sheer spectacle, unable to recognise a single participant thanks to the coating of gloop covering every feature, unassisted by that commentator who was describing an Eccles cake he had once enjoyed in Lincolnshire, a television motorcycle crashed on the narrow strip of cobbles. There were assorted shouts and curses in gruff French as the stricken pilot, his cameraman and various onlookers formed a scrum trying to right the heavy machine. Then, through the melée, came an English voice imperiously shouting for room

to pass, and a big muddy man stomping on the pedals of his inadequate looking bicycle ploughed through the crowd and off into the middle distance. Before I was aware of it, I was on my feet in the middle of the living room clapping and cheering. It was my first Paris-Roubaix, and I had just encountered Sean Yates.

"I'm a bit worried about this April chapter."
"Why's that?"
"I was reading about Paris-Roubaix last night."
"Don't believe all you read, Phil."
"So I shouldn't believe that though he was good enough to win the thing three times, Johan Museeuw fell off on the cobbles and nearly lost his leg?"
"They're exaggerating."
"Or that when Sean Kelly's mum saw a picture of him after the race she cried?"

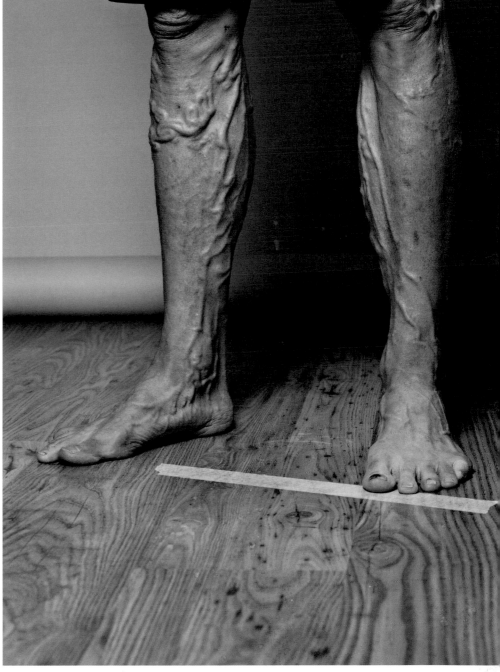

"You know how emotional mothers can be. My mum cries whenever she sees a picture of me."

"Yeah, but that's not distress, that's just disappointment."

"Look, I'll tell you what, why don't we go and see Sean Yates and ask him about it?"

"Oh, what, like you'll just phone him up and say can we come round and see you Sean?"

"Yeah. Hold on... it's ringing... Sean? Hey, it's John. No, John Deering. Yeah, that John. Listen, Phlash and me are thinking of going to do Paris-Roubaix. Can we come over and ask you about it? OK, Thursday? Sweet, see you then."

"Oh my God."

After 15 seasons as a top professional in Europe, Sean Yates is (at the time of writing) the manager, or *directeur sportif* if you prefer, of the biggest budget team in world cycling,

Sky. Amazingly, at some point along that line, I managed to spend a year working with the legend, and we've kept in touch.

"So Phil is a bit worried about Roubaix," I begin.

"You'll be alright," says Sean dismissively. "You've ridden the cobbles before haven't you?"

"Yeah, we've just done Flanders," says Phil

Above: *Sean Yates. These legs have seen a lot of action. Don't try this at home.*

"Ah. Well, they're not like that in France. They're bigger and more knackered. But there aren't any hills. So that's good for you," replies Sean, with a meaningful look in my direction.

"What advice would you give us about the pavé?"

"At Roubaix? Ride along the crown of the road. That's how you can tell who's going well, they don't bother to look for the flattest bit, or the edge of the road. They just smash it straight down the middle."

Neither of us has the bottle to mention his legs. At 51, his varicose veined shins are like a relief map of footpaths around Scafell Pike. Phil shoots off a couple of snaps when he thinks the tall guy's not looking.

"Are you going to Roubaix this year Sean?"

"Nah, I'm off to Tenerife on a training camp with the guys who are riding the Tour de France.

They're not going to Roubaix. It's too specialist these days. In the old days, everybody used to have to do it, no choice."

"You liked it though, didn't you?"

"Yeah, it was my biggest day of the year. I got fifth once, had some other years when I rode in the front most of the day, too. But you either need a lot of luck or to be super, super strong to win Roubaix, and I wasn't lucky enough or strong enough. But I loved doing it. For once I got to be the leader and the others had to fetch bottles for me instead of the other way round. Tell you what, when are you going?"

"We're going to head out a couple of days before the actual event and ride the course if we can."

"I'll ring the guys that are going. See if you can hook up with them for a bit of advice."

"Result. Thanks, legs. I mean veins. I mean Sean. Thanks Sean."

"No problem."

Below: A special race demands special tyres. Many riders choose tubulars made specifically for this one event.

Opposite: Not just a line. Also a pocket. Sky: controlling the controllables.

This is the line

The line between winning and losing

Between failure and success

Between good and great

Between dreaming and believing

Between convention and innovation

Between head and heart

It's a fine line

It challenges everything we do

And we ride it every

igmarkets.com

It's early April 2012. Despite getting to Kortrijk an hour before we needed to, we're now late because we can't find Sky's hotel. We've been steered wrong a couple of times by well-meaning but clueless locals. Finally, flustered and breathless, we're parking up outside a rather well-heeled building tucked away close to the city's medieval central square.

"Wow. Shall we stay here tonight?"

"We may need to flog a few of our imaginary books first."

"Look, there's Edvald Boasson Hagen. He's, like, really good. And Juan Antonio Flecha. He's bloody brilliant. And Jeremy Hunt. He's English. Let's talk to him."

"Alright Jez. I'm John and this is Phil. Sean sent us to have a ride with you today."

"Cool."

We put our kit on.

"That didn't go badly at all. Go back and ask him about the cobbles."

"OK."

"So, Jez, what's your trick to riding the cobbles?"

"Why, are you guys doing Roubaix?"

"Err... yeah, that's the plan."

"Christ, good luck."

"Thanks."

We look at each other.

"Try another one of them."

"Alright."

"Hi Juan-Antonio, I'm John. Sean sent us."

"Hi. Everybody calls me Flecha." He says it like Ronnie Barker in *Porridge*.

"What's your secret to riding the cobbles?"

"I just pretend they're not there."

"Pretend they're not there. I like that."

"Why, are you guys doing Roubaix?"

"Yes."

"Good luck."

Below: Chris Sutton and Edvald Boasson Hagen get the benefit of a Deering pep talk.

When we roll out of the hotel in a 12-strong group, we head for the smooth traffic-free canal paths that abound in this part of the world. Judging from the many groups we see passing, this is a very popular way of training between races for the pros. We're doing 20mph steady, which is about a quarter quicker than I'm used to, but we're whistling along easily in a slipstream because we all ride two millimetres away from the wheel in front. This is scary, not just because we might crash, but I can see the headlines: *Flecha To Miss Roubaix After Training Accident With English Prat.*

I find myself alongside Aussie Chris Sutton. I resist the temptation to ask him why he was such a flop at Chelsea, assuming that he, like most people, wouldn't find this amusing. Instead, he actually gives me some advice about the cobbles. "The key thing is not to hold the bars too tight. That's the biggest mistake people make. Your brain is telling you to hang on for dear life, you grit your teeth, your arms go rigid and your hands feel like you're holding the rope in tug-o-war. You've got to make yourself relax. Some people like to push a bigger gear, but I tend to spin my feet faster and try to float over them. It works for me," he shrugs.

After two hours, a coffee and a cream cake, we're back at the hotel. We know everything there is to know about pavé, kaissen, setts and cobbles. We're going to Paris-Roubaix.

Allez!

We're here a couple of days before the race itself. The route, which has marginal changes from year to year, has already been laid out and signposted for the weekend. This is lucky, as we will discover that some of the roads don't really look like roads at all, and the route takes some pretty improbable directions as it twists and

Below: *Pep talk over, the Sky team now feel the benefit of Deering's awesome power.*

turns to find every piece of busted surface in northern France.

It has been many years since Paris-Roubaix actually started in Paris. By modern standards, the original nineteenth century distance of over 300km isn't practical for a one-day event, so in labouring steps the start made its way to Compiègne, a town about 60km north-east of Paris. In 2012, the race was 258km long. That involves about 100km of nothingness to start with, so Phil and I have decided to begin our Paris-Roubaix mission at Troisvilles, the first section of pavé, 100 miles separating us from the finish on the velodrome in Roubaix.

It's always been a race about the cobbles, but in 1896, when it began, that's because cobbles were what roads were made out of. After the war, villages and towns began tarmacing their roads in earnest. By the 1970s, the race was in severe danger of losing its character, as local authorities and mayors saw the race as bringing shame on their towns by exposing their poor roads. To counter this, some enterprising people set up a society to seek out the old cobbled pathways and tracks that joined these villages together and protect them for the future well-being of the race. That's how we find ourselves in Troisville on a grey morning.

"There's nothing here."

"No, there isn't is there? Come on. Let's get it done."

In retrospect, 100km of warming up wouldn't have been the worst preparation for the pavé. We are immediately bouncing like ten-year olds in the back of the school minibus as we race to get to yet another school football match. Chris Sutton's voice rings in my head as I try to loosen my hold on the bars, but it's easier said than done. As for his floating over the cobbles, all I can say is that he is, of course, a far better cyclist than me. I opt for the other approach.

Below: Paris-Roubaix riders experimented with suspension in the 1990s but have returned to using technique over technology.

I shift the chain into a harder gear and concentrate on churning the pedals round. In this way I take more of my weight on my feet, and my bum almost hovers on the saddle rather than sits right on it.

The last great French cyclist, Bernard Hinault, dismissed Paris-Roubaix as nothing more than a cyclo-cross race. He turned up, won it, and never came back. What a dude.

It soon becomes apparent that this part of the world isn't quite as flat as it looks on TV. In a car, the slow folds of the bleak countryside would be almost imperceptible. On smooth Surrey roads, you wouldn't need to change gear. But on an uphill drag on battered pavé, a moment's rest can be fatal. It's essential that you keep firing yourself forward, hammering the pedals toward the low grey skyline. Momentum is everything.

The shape of the roads themselves is bizarre. Centuries of cart wheels and tractor tyres have produced deep sunken trenches on either side of a high crown that sometimes sprouts grass. Driving a family car along here would almost certainly result in a hearty expensive thwack on the sump. The options for bike riders are to plough along the centre on the raised apex, or look for a way through the dirt and dust at the side of the road. Though that part is invariably smoother, every so often it will run out, forcing you into a deep ditch or a pothole like a dustbin. Avoiding these takes you back into the deep ruts you sought to avoid in the first place. I don't think there's a right answer to this conundrum. We just do the best we can.

Phil's lighter body seems to be taking more of a battering than mine. He climbs very well, but it's becoming clear that in terrain like this, the momentum of my bulk is actually an asset. We try riding on the drops, riding on the hoods, riding on the tops. It's all awful, really.

When I was 15, I went to see Motorhead at Hammersmith Odeon. I was right near the

Above: The sections of pavé come thick and fast as the route travels further north.

front. The volume was like nothing I'd ever experienced. It never slackened off, assaulting my senses and continually pounding me until I became numb to the noise. When I came out into the night afterwards, there was a strange calm in the world around me, but an outraged insistent buzzing inside me that lasted for days. That feeling comes back to me each time we exit a section of pavé and find ourselves on twenthieth-century roads again. My whole body is alive as every atom in it screams, but outside all is calm.

After mile upon mile of grey-brown fields, grey-brown towns and grey-brown roads, huge hulking derricks loom up out of the gloom. These are the mine workings of Wallers Arenberg, and they mark the entrance to the hardest part of the road to Roubaix, the Arenberg Forest. It was here that the Flemish master, Johan Museuuw, hit the ground so hard that his kneecap burst under the impact. The wound became infected and for a while it was thought that his leg would need to be amputated. He shrugged that off and got back on his bike. Two years later he was first off the cobbles and on to the Roubaix track, crossing the line with one leg outstretched, his index finger pointing markedly at the knee that had nearly lost him everything in one of sport's most memorable victory salutes.

Below: Much of the route of Paris-Roubaix runs through the traditional heart of French coal-mining territory.

A long, straight dark track leads into the trees. Hansel and Gretel may well have come this way. If they had, the breadcrumbs they dropped to retrace their steps would probably still be here, as I haven't seen a hint of avian life at any point during the 80km since Troisvilles. This is it: the Trouée d'Arenberg.

cattle grid, and the bars are grotesquely bent upwards and misshapen. Imagine that feeling that if you so much as turn your handlebars one degree in either direction, your wheel will disappear between the gaps in these bars and all will be lost. Now imagine that going on for two miles.

Imagine having to get off on a flat road. There is a smooth footpath over to our right. I snatch a longing glance at it, but knowing this will be behind barriers on race day, we resolve to stick to the purpose of our mission and drive on. Fools.

Regaining solid ground at last, we look at each other in silence. Then, gradually, a laugh builds up from somewhere, gurgling in our throats and forcing its way out into the cold spring air. Eventually, we are giggling giddily like three-year-olds on Tizer.

"Shall we go back and do it again?"

"Shall I punch you in the face?"

"Tell you what, though."

"What?"

"Only 80km to go."

"I don't give a monkey's. They can't be as hard as that."

And do you know what? They aren't. Beating Arenberg has crowned us Kings of the Cobbles. The sun shows its bleary hungover face.

Above: *The centre of the Hell of the North, Arenberg. This is the most difficult section of the event.*

Next page: *The experts advise riding along the crest of the pavé to avoid the worst ruts.*

Even the Nord-Pas-de-Calais doesn't look so inhospitable now. We laugh at the grimness of the power stations and the one-donkey towns and villages. We skip over the pavé. We pass routemarkers planted in enormous piles of manure. They have a sense of humour.

Phil – I'll tell you what the difference is between Belgium and France: Belgium is neater. Their gardens are immaculate, the hedges are trimmed to within a centimetre of their lives. Their houses, rebuilt after a century of destruction and more destruction, look like something out of Toytown. Here in France, just over the border and a short ride from where we were in March, everything is a bit scruffy in comparison. I prefer that.

The Carrefour de l'Arbre section of cobbles is really truly bad, but having seen this race so many times on the telly, we know that we're at the business end and it doesn't matter now. We're dragging up the long busy avenue into Roubaix itself before the afternoon is done.

"I don't remember Boonen having to stop at all these traffic lights."

"It's OK, nobody in London seems to stop for them either."

Finally, I'm sticking out my knee and we're sweeping into the velodrome. We had talked about how we were going to get into the old stadium, whether we should bring wirecutters or be ready to climb gates and fences. We shouldn't have worried: it's open. A scrubby football pitch is surrounded by a beige concrete bike track, complete with modest banking at either end. A couple of unimpressed joggers do laps. The stand looks like the sort of stand that should never have the prefix grand. This is where the world's greatest one-day bike race ends. Who would believe it?

We swing right on to the track, half of the lap to cover before we hear the imaginary bell. At this point in Roubaix, the gladiators still left in the fight are testing their tired limbs, flexing their fingers, wondering if their hamstrings will take one last push without cramping up.

Opposite: *Sometimes you have to pause for a moment just to get some life back into your limbs.*

Above: *One arrow. One pile of manure. Imaginative route assistance on the road to Roubaix.*

Will they be able to hold their nerve, Lester Piggott-like, to produce their steeds in the final few yards, or will they feel forced to throw themselves out into the wind from a lap out, nerves jangling and shredded in a desperate but obviously ill-conceived gamble to be first? Will they cross the line inseparable in a sprint like Steve Bauer and Eddy Planckaert, only for the Belgian to inexplicably be given the benefit of the doubt in what should surely have been called a dead heat?

I give Phil my best cold-eye stare and take the upper part of the banking, trying to look cool while thinking that it looks a bit precarious from up here. He glares dead ahead and begins to lift the pace. As we enter the final corner, I realise my mistake: I can't sprint flat out from up here, it's too steep and I feel a bit unstable. He pulls

out a couple of bike lengths on me and it's all or nothing. I swoop down the banking, rocketing into the final straight and inch past him to take the greatest victory of my long and illustrious career. My first Paris-Roubaix. A jogger looks at me with absolute disgust.

Back in Troisvilles, on the very first section of pavé, I had stopped on a corner. I'd noticed a bit of blackened earth where somebody had been

burning stuff raked off from the neighbouring fields. In the remains of the fire, a lump had caught my eye: a red-brown piece of what looked like brick. I nudged it with my toe and it rolled over. It was a Paris-Roubaix cobble. I put it in my jersey pocket and carried it with me all the way to the velodrome. Now I take it out and hold it aloft, like Kelly, like Hinault, like de Vlaeminck, like Museeuw, like Boonen.

Above: Head to head in the world's favourite velodrome. There could be only one winner.

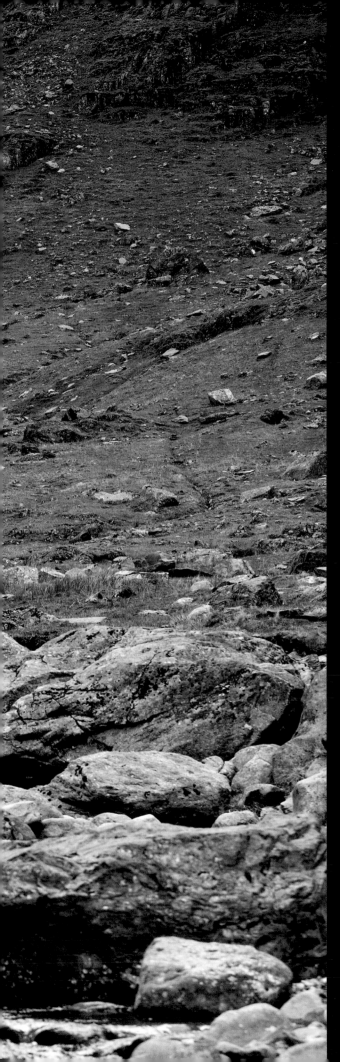

May

Fred Whitton Challenge

"What's the most pathetic job you can think of?"
"Hmm. Let me think. I presume you're asking this because you've already thought of one?"
"Yeah."
"Go on then."
"Royal watcher. As in, 'we're joined this morning on the sofa by a renowned royal watcher...' I mean, royal correspondent is a pretty pathetic job for somebody aspiring to be a serious journalist, but royal watcher? It's not even as if you're employed, is it? 'The Queen wore a blue dress, whereas at this event last year, she wore a green one.' I don't care."

We don't like people, us. Me and Phil. Miserable old gits. Him very slightly older than me, but both miserable, and both gits. That's the problem with all these mass participation things: it's the whole "mass" thing. In fact, "participation" in general, come to think of it. I hate participating. We're not even the worst in our little gang. You should meet some of the friends we go riding with. Wow. They really don't like people. But I just told you that to make us look slightly less gittish. We're just as bad, truth be told. Which makes things like the Fred Whitton difficult for us. Well, to be honest, it's the 112 miles and the 13,000ft of climbing that makes it difficult, but whatever.

It's six o'clock in the morning and I'm standing among a bunch of excitable middle-aged men in lycra. I too, by definition, am a middle-aged man in lycra, but I am not excitable or excited. I am apprehensive and a miserable old git, as we have established. Another middle-aged man in lycra who is also an apprehensive miserable old git is taking my picture. At least we have each other.

Left: *Honister Pass, one of six huge obstacles in the Fred Whitton Challenge.*

Above: *Approaching the summit of Kirkstone Pass, linking Windermere to Ullswater.*

"We know where the roads go. We know that people have spent a long time deciding on how this route will hang together. Why do we have to ride it at the same time as all these other people?"

"It's an event. That's what you do."

"It's not what we do."

"OK. This will be the last one. Promise."

"Apart from next month?"

"Apart from next month."

We had a nice dinner in a pub in Coniston last night. We were surrounded by cyclists, so we puffed out our bellies, swigged many beers and pretended to be motorcyclists. We don't like people. Did I mention that?

Fred Whitton, from what we can understand after talking to people who knew him, was a bloody good bloke. Definitely not a miserable old git. He was virtually single-handedly the face of cycling in the Lakes, no small feat in itself. When he unexpectedly left this world in 1998 at the stupidly young age of 50, he left a massive hole, which his friends filled by organising this event. In short order, it has become the must-ride event for Britain's burgeoning sportive crowd. Have you got a Lakeophile in the family? Maybe somebody who spends their weekends in big boots, knocking off the Dale Head Round before breakfast, going up Watendlath over Glaramara and back over Arsengarthenthwaite and Scafell Pike on one leg? If you tell them you're going to ride your bike over Kirkstone Pass, Honister Pass, Newlands Pass, Whinlatter Pass, Hardknott Pass and Wrynose Pass, even these battle-hardened Lakeland veterans will raise a weatherbeaten knotty eyebrow. Then tell them you'll do it in one day and they'll raise the other one. Like Roger Moore gone wrong.

Sneaky in the extreme. The first climb on this ride, a hoik over unnamed hills between Coniston and Hawkshead. My God. Too soon.

By the time we arrive shivering in Ambleside, accompanied by gibbering fools with their

Above: *Borrowdale spring lambs smile obligingly for the camera.*

saddles too low, heads too noddy, bikes too creaky and voices way too loud, I am deeply unhappy. At least they don't take us up The Struggle, an aptly named lane that runs out of the back of Ambleside and comes out on to Kirkstone Pass-proper near the summit. Instead we're going the long way round to reach our first nominated obstacle of the day.

When I was 22, I had my one and only serious bike accident. A lady driving an Austin Montego (it was that long ago, don't laugh), saw that she had about ten seconds before the next car came down the hill towards her, so quickly executed a right-hand turn. Unfortunately, she nearly executed me too, as I was riding my bike in that very spot and she hadn't been looking out for cyclists. I crushed two vertebrae in my back and broke my shoulder. I like to tell people that this incident ended my promising racing career, but that's disgracefully disingenuous, as decent bike riders recover from things like that all the time. It did,

however, leave me with a propensity for back trouble that happens to flare up unannounced at inopportune moments. Like a mile from the top of the Kirkstone Pass, for instance.

I've gone a long way to incorporate some safeguards to this happening. I use a compliant Giant carbon monocoque frame. I set the bike up to a forgiving sportive position. I follow a programme of exercises to strengthen my core muscles. What I don't do is eat a bit less, which would probably help.

As it happens, I get over the top of Kirkstone without significant difficulty, then prepare for the long fast descent to Ullswater. It's still early in the morning, and pretty nippy up here, but the road is wide and smooth, so I shoot down, overtaking some of the skinny types that passed me on the way up. It's only when I get down to the lake that I realise I have something of a problem developing. Now that I need to pedal, I'm getting a sharp pinching pain in my lower back just above the hip as I turn the pedal over the top of its revolution.

"You don't look happy. I mean, even less happy than usual. Even less happy than earlier."

"I'll be OK, keep rolling, I'm going to take it easy for a mile or two."

"Easier than usual?"

"Very funny."

As Phil coasts off, I go through a routine of stretches while rolling along, trying to free my back of the spasm. It feels a bit better. Just by Aira Force waterfall, we swing left to pass over another hill that will take us up to Troutbeck on the north western corner of the route. My attempts to push on up the hill are greeted by a sudden yelp that comes out of my mouth and my hands leave the bars for a second in shock. I've seemingly been stabbed by somebody from C-Block carrying a shiv and sticking me in the back for being a grass. I roll the pedals round more gently and the pain subsides, but I'm now going embarrassingly slowly. Phil has pulled over to get some shots a little higher up. I know it must look bad because he's not laughing at me.

By the time we're trudging along the horrible windswept stretch of trunk road that will take us into Keswick, I'm weighing up my options. Once we leave the town, there will be no real turning back, as the central Lakeland fells can't be crossed to make a shortcut back to base. It's turn left in Keswick and crawl back to Coniston alone and defeated, or smash myself to bits completing the entire course. I'd like to say that I begged Phil to let me carry on, had to be sternly talked out of such madness and was left with no option but to abandon. I'd like to say that, but I can't.

"I'm going to have to pack."

"No big sprint victory this time then?"

"No big sprint victory."

"Drive for show, putt for dough?"

"Something like that."

"Fair enough. Will you get back alright?"

"I'll see you there."

"OK, be careful."

And then there was one.

Phil – To be honest, I was on the verge of going back with him. I was hating it. The A66 was a low point in my cycling year: headwinds, juggernauts, long drags. They were forecasting rain by lunchtime and the bright start to the day had disappeared into something altogether more grey. But I knew how annoyed I would be if I didn't have a proper crack at it. And after all, my back wasn't hurting, so I wouldn't even have an excuse.

The bottom of Honister Pass is really steep. I mean really steep. There's no clue to which way you'll climb out of Borrowdale when you're rolling along the valley floor. In fact, the most likely route looks like the valley of Seathwaite, butted at its far end by the massive hump of Great End, stopping you from seeing Scafell behind it. But when you reach the hamlet of Seatoller, you take a right instead, and all of a sudden everything is 25 percent up. Some people are tacking backwards and forwards across the road like yachts into the wind. I'm glad I put a lower gear on the back: I'm in it immediately, and stay in it all the way up. My saving grace is that Honister is quite a "rampy" climb. You can afford to go into the red to get up the steepest bits as it will ease slightly before too long. A horror, nevertheless.

It's quickly becoming apparent that the rest of this ride, beautiful as it may be, will be all about the hardship. I'm not a Lakeland afficionado, but still know that Newlands, Whinlatter, Hardknott and Wrynose Passes are going to be significant obstacles, and I've only gone over two named hills so far. I'd like to get to know this part of the world better really, but preferably with Jane and Emily in a comfortable car on a sunny day outside the school holidays and without 3,000 gurning clubbies around me.

That said, Newlands Pass is undeniably beautiful. Not one of the most renowned of the big climbs (I hadn't heard of it, anyway), it starts on a very steep little mountain road by the pastoral church in Buttermere. Once you've actually struggled up and over the windy gap at the summit, the true gentle splendour of Newlands Valley opens up: rolling rough fields surrounded by high crags. I could live here, I reckon, and store that away to tell John later. He's always banging on about where you would live if you could live anywhere.

We came over Whinlatter Pass in the other direction in the winter when we were doing the C2C. To be honest, I don't remember it being as horrible as this. It's similar to Honister in that it ramps up violently out of a little village, but it seems to go on forever. It's not as cold as then – I distinctly remember a couple of "moments" caused by ice on the way down here in January – but it's not what you'd call warm. One of the reasons we made such an early start was that they're forecasting rain for later, but the moment it's grey, chilly, grey, damp, grey and there's a westerly starting to blow up. It turns into a bit of a hooley as we

are led out of the Lakes proper and on to the exposed moorland above Sellafield. Insert your own mutant joke here. All I can tell you is that it was as horrible a part of this ride as any, despite the fact that there were no listed passes to worry about. Just hard, draggy, windswept hillside with nothing to see apart from a miserable great power station.

By the time we finally swing into Eskdale and the comfort of a following wind I am well and truly knackered. I reckon this has already become the longest day in the saddle this year, and the two highest passes are still in front of me.

I'm going to spend a bit of time telling you about Hardknott Pass, as it is a serious contender for hardest road in England. What a great name, for starters. About half way up this monster – you're starting pretty much from sea level and clearing 1,289ft eventually – there's a Roman Fort, and it was these pioneers that stuck the road in, the best part of 2,000 years ago. Imagine being garrisoned there in the third century. You're from a decent family in the south of Italy somewhere, growing up among olive groves and lemon trees, an ambitious young soldier on the up, and you get sent here.

Previous page: Down to Brothers Water. One pass covered, five to go, plus countless smaller hills.

Right: Eskdale from the lower part of Hardknott Pass. The Roman fort here was one of the lesser-favoured postings for a legionary.

The temperature never gets above ten degrees. It's always raining. It's always windy. Celtic people are trying to kill you on a daily basis. Best of all, you're wearing a skirt. My God.

The first set of hairpins as you exit the lush oak woods at the bottom are steep enough to have you seriously thinking about the best line on the corners. Go round the outside and take a longer route, or bully your way up the crazy ramps on the inside? It's hard to know what's best. Lots of people are using really, really low gears, and I wonder if I went low enough. It gradually dawns on me, however, that you can actually get too low. I can hear clicking in front of me, and in a few seconds I know why... Christ on a Chopper, would you look at that... there's a straight pitch up, not on a bend, but a straight bit of road for God's sake, that is steeper than anything else I've seen. Ever. People are clicking out of their pedals and shaking their heads in disbelief, totally

understandable when you think that we've already been on our absolute limits for the last 15 minutes anyway. This is where I realise that too low thing is true: if I changed down, I would have nothing left to push against. As it is, this is more like stepping than bike riding, just putting one foot painfully in front of the other, fighting to roll the gear over and not stop. Don't stop. Don't stop. After a few minutes of thinking that every pedal step will be the last, the gradient finally backs off and I think for the first time: I will make this.

I just looked up Hardknott on Wikipedia and found that it vies with Rosedale Chimney in Yorkshire for the title of England's Steepest Road. They both have sections at 33 percent. I won't be seeking out Rosedale Chimney any time soon.

I'm a bit wobbly over the top. It's hard to eat and drink enough on the Fred Whitton as you're either struggling up a massive hill or hanging on for grim death down the other side.

Opposite: *Hardknott Pass is one of Britain's steepest roads, bullying the bike rider with a 33 percent gradient.*

Below: *With Hardknott done, only Wrynose remains between your front wheel and a cup of tea.*

Right: A well-earned rest. You might not call the hardship of the Fred Whitton fun, but it's still a great achievement to finish.

The best thing about the wild crazily steep descent off of Hardknott is that there is a friendly face waiting for me at the bottom. And when he manages to unfold his complaining spine to open the back of the car, he's made me a ham and cheese roll too. Good lad.

"Nice. Thanks."

"That's OK. I think you've earned it."

"So, regretting going back?"

"Not really."

"Regretting being outclassed?"

"I'm injured. I had no choice. It was like Bryan Robson's shoulder."

"Chin up. See you at the finish."

It's hard to tear myself away across the barren watershed that separates Hardknott and Wrynose, but I'm on the last leg now. In theory, Wrynose is just as hard as Hardknott, being exactly the same height and having similar super-steep bits, but I can see as I head towards its foot

that it doesn't provide anything like as much of an obstacle from this side. The main reason for its comparative ease is that you actually lose very little height off Hardknott, so you're basically starting from near the top. Suits me just fine.

There's still half an hour of upping and downing, but the organisers have employed some very thoughtful nearly-there type signs for the run in to keep the weary traveller's spirits up. Mine are definitely up. That was the hardest day ever on a bike by some distance. And I didn't walk once. Hooray for me.

"Well done superstar. Do you want a sausage roll?"

"Do you want to lick my face?"

"Not really, but I recognise the sentiment. I acknowledge that you are better than me and you have won. Today."

"That's sorted, then. Now, what did you say about a sausage roll?"

June

Dragon Ride

"What was that thing you said the other day? You know, the funny thing?"

"What funny thing?"

"You said something funny and we said we ought to remember it, put it in the book."

"I can't remember."

"Come on, it's not like it happens that often."

"What do you mean by that?"

"Well, you know, if it was me that had said it, we wouldn't have to worry about remembering it, because there'll be another one along in a minute."

"That's outrageous."

"I'm the funny one. You're my straight man."

"Yeah, right. I'm no more an Ernie than you're an Eric."

"My stooge."

"How about I jam a screwdriver into your gums?"

"Philips or flat blade?"

"It would be my screwdriver, so Philips."

"Ah! See! You can do it. I knew another funny would come along eventually. Well done you."

"Right, that's it. Where's my toolbox..."

It's reasonable to say that the Dragon Ride splits opinion. As Britain's biggest sportive, and the only internationally ratified British event, it's certainly a landmark on the calendar. Some find the huge start area, miles of crowd barriers and cheering sponsor-supplied rent-a-crowd inspiring and the stamp of a big event. Some find it patronising, over the top and more than faintly ridiculous for an amiable bike ride. I'll leave you to figure out which camp Phlash and I are likely to fall into.

Left: *Looking across to Fforest Fawr, bathed in Welsh sunshine. The north side of the Dragon Ride provides spectacular panoramas.*

For instance, at the start, in the capacious rolling parkland of Margham Park, there are two clowns. Real ones, not THESE two clowns, thank you very much at the back. One of them is on stilts, the other one is riding a tricycle powered by bubbles. I have a good, long look round as they wend their way through the hordes gathering on the line, and reckon that there is virtually nobody here under the age of 30, let alone six. Maybe I'm just cynical and jaded, but I'm just not as entertained by clowns as I once was. At best they're incongruous, at worst they put the fear of God into coulrophobics trying to occupy their minds by riding bikes instead of having nightmares about men wearing make-up in the style of Barbara Cartland and driving old cars that hilariously fall apart when one blows the outdated horn.

We roll out past a huge starters gantry, possibly borrowed from Silverstone, cheered on by identically dressed grinning automatons.

"Well done!"
"Good luck!"
"Well done!"
Whatever.

Now here's the surprising part. The route of Britain's biggest sportive is truly awful. Quick set of directions for you: turn left on to grim residential street. Pass through town where people commit suicide as regularly as going to the shops. Do 20 miles along grey suburban roads. Do another 20 miles along greyer suburban roads. Hard right at the boarded up shops. Up a two-mile dead straight hill on a road as wide as the Thames. Through a village built 60 years ago and abandoned 20 years ago. And so on.

If you like your roads without lines down the middle, don't come here.

To be fair, choosing the middle distance route may have been, for once, a mistake. The longer

Below: Concrete set against moorland is a recurring theme for long stretches of the Dragon Ride.

Gran Fondo (Welsh for longer) route takes in some smaller lanes around the far part of the course, scaling some steep hills in the Brecon Beacons National Park. We're restricted to 40 miles of concrete jungle followed by 20 miles of big climbs on A-roads then another 20 miles of dross.

I don't really understand it. There's some beautiful roads round here and some stunning backdrops. Why won't they let us see them? Conversation returns to a familiar topic.

"So how's the great trim up going?"
"I haven't gone for the full razor treatment yet. When I've got the clippers out, after doing my head, I run them up and down my legs too."
"Working towards it? Baby steps?"
"Sort of."
"You sound uncomfortable with this?"
"Well."
"So what does Jane say about it?"
"Yeah, that."
"Ohhh, I see."

The climb of Rhigos is quite impressive. A long, straight drag past abandoned mine workings hauls you up out of the valleys before a series of switchbacks across windswept mountainside delivers you to a windy ridge high above South Wales. It's a plod for me to say the least.

"So... err... how do I put this..."
"Spit it out, man."
"When you shave, how far up do you go? Just to the short line?"

Right: *There are obvious reasons why towns sprang up in these valleys.*

Above: *A local hostelry fails to capture the attention of the descending field of riders.*

Opposite: *Rhigos summit. The bulk of miles may be behind you now, but there are still some heavy roads ahead.*

"No, that's the best bit, the bit under your shorts. When you take them off at the end of a long day, there's a real relief that there's been no rubbing and pulling or soreness on your thighs."

"So where, then?"

"It just sort of dies out at the top. I don't draw a line, there's a natural stopping point."

"Hmm. Yeah. That's the problem. I'm hairier than you, it just carries on."

legs, finishing in a neat line either side of my groin."

"The reason being?"

"Naked, it would be like I was wearing a pair of hair pants."

"Genius. Do it."

"No."

There's a very different crowd here to the Fred

types and a much higher proportion of women than we've run into at previous events, and that gives the crowd a more upbeat feel than we've come across before. Except us, obviously, the miserable old gits. I'm so bored. I don't remember wishing I'd brought my iPod on one of these before.

On the way down Rhigos to Treorchy, we pass a bizarre area I can only describe as a garden. But it's three-quarters of the way up a most unlovely scree-covered mountain. There are multicoloured little works of art scattered about like tributes to distant mountain gods, driven

out of South Wales by the arrival of the pits and now licking their wounds in the Himalayas.

Not far now. The boarded-up pebble-dashed two-up-two-downs are leading us home.

"You know I'm staying at Mum and Dad's at the moment?"

"Yes?"

"I got back late the other night, so I stopped at Tesco's on the way in, picked up a pizza, some salad, whatnot."

"Right."

"I like to liven the old supermarket pizza up

Above: Descending at speed into the Rhondda Valley. With roads big enough to have white lines down the middle, you can afford to let go.

a bit, you know, bit of buffala, chopped chillis, sprig of rocket, that sort of thing."

"Always a winner."

"Yeah. Anyway, it was nice, though the little chilli was a bit hotter than I'd expected."

"That's a really interesting story."

"Wait. That's not it."

"Oh?"

"Later on, I went for a wee. And I did that thing you shouldn't do."

"What? What thing? Did you... oh-ho-ho, wait a minute... you didn't touch the old boy with your chilli fingers did you?"

"Yep."

"Ah, that's brilliant. That's made my day."

"Excruciating. Like somebody had a lit match on it. Stop laughing.

"I can't. You'll have to wait for me. What did you do?"

"I ran the sink full of of cold water and dropped it in."

"Ha!"

"I was standing there, waiting for blessed relief to arrive, then had a sudden thought... did I bolt the door?"

"Your Mum walks in to find you with your tackle in her bathroom sink?"

Oh look. There are the grinning people again.

"Well done!"

"Brilliant!"

"Well done!"

"Congratulations!"

Sigh. Oh no, please. You really can't be serious. A medal.

And there's a band on. A pub band doing Eric Clapton. Frankly, I don't need it.

The Dragon Ride. Britain's most challenging sportive, or tedium on two-wheels? Plenty of people we met this weekend think the former. Come and decide for yourselves.

Opposite: *The Dragon Ride is Britain's biggest sportive, attracting a broader spread of entries than most.*

Below: *The hills string out the field but most of the Dragon Ride's climbing is on major roads.*

Next page: *Across Treorchy from Bwlch to distant Pen-y-Fan. The Dragon's character is found in its juxtaposition of urban spread and wild beauty.*

July

Bealach na Ba

It turns out that I don't need a match. My teeny little Calor gas stove actually lights itself, and in a few minutes my camping kettle is whistling a merry tune. Coffee works well in the open air, and you don't get much more open air than this. We're looking out over the calm blue of the Inner Sound with the raw hills of Applecross behind us and the jagged Mordor peaks of Skye's Cuillins reflected in the water. It's the sort of morning that makes you want to believe in an almighty something or other.

Around this beautiful ragged peninsula, more like an island than many of the islands, lies one of Britain's most scenic roads. My 1982 version of W.A. Poucher's *Guide to the Scottish Peaks* says, "The new road encircling the Applecross Peninsula has now been completed. The engineering of the road is marvellous and has a smooth tarmac surface." In parts, it doesn't look like it's been surfaced since the famous climber and guide (who had an unusual and amusing penchant for wearing the Yardley cosmetics he also sold) came this way, but it's none the worse for it. We're here to ride this new road.

By linking up to the "mainland" at Shieldag and heading up Glen Torridon, we're making a 90-mile loop. A great ride for a summer's day, and no chance of getting caught out after dark. In these latitudes in early July, evening lasts from about 7pm until midnight. You might be waking up early if you leave the tent flaps open, though.

The entire ride is soaked in glorious scenery, but there is one obstacle in particular waiting for us. To find our way back to our starting point in Applecross, we'll have to grapple with Scotland's highest pass.

Left: Across the Inner Sound to the Cuillins. There is hardly a yard on this road that doesn't have a stunning view.

At over 2,000ft, the Bealach na Ba, or Pass of the Cattle, or Cow Pass, takes some beating. There are two great sportive rides, both run by the lovely Hands On people, that take in the Bealach. We're doing the route of the Mhor, or Greater, while there is also a Beag. At only 40 miles, the Beag is certainly not to be sniffed at in terms of either difficulty or grandiosity as it loops the Applecross peninsula. Both the Hands On rides usually start up at the northern end of the loop, but we want to start in Applecross itself, meaning the mighty climb will be scaled just before the end.

"Coffee tastes so good when you've made it yourself outdoors, eh? What is it?"
"Only Lavazza Red."
"Well it's really good."
"Must be the barista's technique."
"Must be."

The sunshine is beautiful and warm as we rise gently above the bay, Applecross's neat white houses looking out towards us down to our left. At the left hand end of the line, we can just make out the tables outside the Applecross Inn where we devoured some very fine haddock last night. Pre-event carb loading. We could have gone for pre-event crab loading, but the haddock came with chips. There's a chilly northerly breeze blowing in from the Arctic across The Minch this morning, making the hair on my bare arms stand up. We head further north, sun on our backs, over a succession of sharp little rises on a grippy beige single track road. The distant height of An Cliseam over the sea in Lewis rears gradually over the sharp horizon. It's a beautiful day.

"Doesn't sound very Scottish, does it?"
"What doesn't?"

Above: *Clambering up to the northern end of the Applecross peninsula. The road that links the scattered crofts was only completed 40 years ago.*

Opposite: *The incessant climbing and descending means many rank the longer route around Applecross harder than the Bealach itself.*

"Applecross."

"Oh, right. They don't know exactly where it's from, but they think it's an anglicisation of some old Scottish words. Aber an Crossan, mouth of the River Crossan, they reckon."

"Right. I'll try that one out in the Aber an Crossan Inn tonight, see how I get on."

We're a bit late in the season to see the masses of gannets that dive this coastline in the spring. They say they all live in the far north, mainly on Handa Island, then plough their way up and down the west coast following fish. In the north, the gannets themselves are invariably followed by one or two skuas, the gangsters of the cliffs. I once saw two skuas follow a gannet until it caught a fish, then they jumped it. One flew off with the booty whilst the other one held the law-abiding bird under the water until it went limp. Dog eat dog. Or rather, dog eat poor innocent rabbit. Instead of the gannets,

we see some guillemots, kittiwakes and what might even be puffins, but they're too far out to be sure. And that right there, just diving in that little bay, is our fifth shag of the weekend. Don't start.

"Alright, here's one for you. Riddle me this."

"Eh?"

"Riddle me this."

"What does that even mean?"

"It means, 'explain this to me.'"

"Why don't you say that then?"

"Alright, OK. Explain this to me."

"I'm all ears.

"Drinking that coffee on the beach this morning reminded me of something that I wished you'd been there for."

"Always use the Green Cross Code, because I won't be there when you cross the road."

"Alright Dave Prowse, don't change the subject. I was out with this girl the other day and we went into a café."

"Which café?"

"Mambo, if you must know, but it's not important. We –"

"I'll be the judge of that."

"Look, are you going to let me tell this story or not?"

"Go on. Sorry."

"So. We're in this café. I'm having an americano – as people don't know what you're talking about if you ask for a black coffee – she's having a latte."

"You actually have to ask for a black americano now, too."

"I know! Anyway, this chap comes in behind us while we're waiting and orders a cappuccino. Then he says, 'Have you got any croissants?' The girl says, 'Yes.' He says, 'I'll have a croissant too.'"

"Great. So far, so boring."

"Wait. There's a pause, while we're all waiting for the machine. Then he says, 'Are the croissants warm?' And she says, 'Yes, I just took them out of the oven.' Guess what he said then?"

"What?"

"He said, 'Oh, OK, I'll leave it then.'"

"Eh? He asks for a croissant, she says it's warm, and he says that in that case he doesn't want it?"

"Yep. That's it."

"I've never heard anything so ridiculous."

"Me neither. Who would turn down a croissant because it's warm? That's like… that's like… that's not like anything I've ever heard of.

"That's a ludicrous story. I don't believe a word of it."

"What do you mean? Why not?"

"As if a girl would go to a café with you."

As we round the headland we cross rough ground and pass some beautifully wild little lochans. The road turns further easterly and southerly, swivelling the breeze round to rest pleasantly on our shoulders. Deep blue Loch Torridon is down below us, hordes of gulls mobbing a lonesome tiny trawler.

"Is there a better name for a place in the country than Wester Ross? Sounds great, doesn't it?"

"Funnily enough, my favourite county is even further up than this."

"Where's that?"

"Sutherland. The most northerly county in the land is called Sutherland."

"Ross County have got a football team, too. Premier league, no less. I think they're over in Dingwall or somewhere like that. Could Dingwall possibly be a nice place with a name like that? Actually I've been there and it's not bad at all."

"Shall we make them our Scottish team?"

"You've had worse ideas."

Shieldag might well be the most perfect place on the planet. It is this morning, anyway. Boats rest on the calm waters in the lee of a little island, facing a row of whitewashed cottages, a cafe, and a pub. Fortunately it's still early, so we're able to avoid stopping. We may never have left.

Right: Crofters cottages at Kenmore. Long daylight hours and plenty of sunshine dispel the myth of rainy Scotland.

"So answer me this one then, if the Scots get independence, will they get the Euro?"

"The Euro. Oh no."

"I'm just trying to get you going. Explain the Euro crisis to me again?"

"The Euro. Right. Well, here's the thing about the Euro. You've got Germany making all this stuff, decent stuff."

"What sort of stuff?"

"Oh, all sorts of things, but mainly cars."

"Cars?"

"Yeah. Then they think: what if we made it easier for other people to get their hands on all these cars we're making? What if everyone across Europe had the same money as us? Then they could buy more of our stuff."

"I thought the single currency was all about making trading easier for everybody?"

"Yes it is. Especially if you're a German car manufacturer."

"So what's the problem?"

"Well, it's only going to work if everybody's money is worth the same, isn't it? You know, if you're, say, Germany, France or Holland, that's a nice little arrangement. But they want all these aspirational types from Greece, Spain, Portugal and Ireland to buy their cars. So to wrap this up quickly, it's all their fault, greedy sods."

"Where does that leave us then?"

"Well, for all his oddness, Gordon Brown could see that it wasn't a good match for us and kept us out. And in the end, it makes no odds, because if they all go bust, we'll be just as messed up as everybody else."

"I'm getting a new VW then. Save Europe. The Ryder Cup has converted me."

The barren mahoosiveness of Liathach and Beinn Eighe tower over Glen Torridon as we plod along the flat valley away from the treasured coastline. The razor sharp ridge is white with quarzite.

"Hey, I've got another salient fact for you. Remember when Grace Jones attacked Russell Harty?"

"*Televisual gold. Like Del Boy falling through the gap in the bar. Or the elephant treading on John Noakes's foot.*"

"The old boy sitting there looking bemused as she whacked him?"

"*Yes?*"

"None other than W.A. Poucher."

"*No way!*"

"Way."

Below: *Upper Loch Torridon over Shieldag to Liathach. White-tailed eagles nest on islands in the loch.*

Next page: *Scotland's highest pass, the fearsome Bealach na Ba, blocks the route back to Applecross.*

In any other setting, the wide open spaces of Strathcarron would be stunning. Compared to the rest of this ride however, they come across as a little featureless, especially as they accompany a main road, along which we are now trundling back towards our destination. It's not exactly traffic-riddled though, and the anachronistic tiny railway line is a fascination to me. The fact that it has survived depopulation, Dr Beeching and even the road bridge to Skye at Kyle of Lochalsh shows rare depths of tenacity.

"Where would you live if you could live anywhere?"

"I like it here. A lot, actually. I could see me in a little crofter's cottage, waking up to the sun glancing off Loch Torridon, wandering down to the Shieldag Hotel every evening. Weekly drive to Inverness for shopping. Providing employment to the local populace in the form of eating out, drinking out and domestic chores. Yeah, I'd like that."

"Wouldn't you get bored?"

"If I did, I could just go back to London for a few days. Easyjet out of Inverness. Remind me of why I liked it here in the first place."

"I'm loving the fact that it doesn't get dark here. Might be a bit grim in the winter."

"That's why birds fly south. Who am I to buck nature's system?"

"What would you do for work?"

"I'd be independently wealthy."

"That's nice. How, exactly?"

"I'll come back to you on that one. What about you?"

"Ah, I've been meaning to tell you this for ages: Newlands Valley in the north western Lakes."

"Harrumph. You're just saying that because you rode that and I didn't."

"No, it was genuinely amazing. But you'll never know, will you?"

"Double harrumph."

The road swings right and then hard uphill away from Loch Carron, a final warning before the Bealach.

"It's hard to describe, but aren't the skies just bigger up here?"

"I know what you mean. You'd think that flat farmland or open sea ought to give you the biggest skies. Maybe it's the fact that it's framed by big scenery?"

"Perhaps it's not the actual size, how much of it you can see, it's more the way it's lit."

"How do you mean?"

"Well, the sun makes such a long low arc, especially in the evening, it's lighting the sky above rather than the earth below. You know when you're in, say, Florida, or Australia, the light is hard and bright, because the sun's almost overhead?"

"Uh-huh?"

"This is the opposite."

"Right. Like an interior designer uplighting a room?"

"Exactly."

Down past the enticing deck of the Kishorn Seafood Restaurant, past the intimidating sign that basically says: Bealach na Ba – Don't Come Up Here, and we're on it. Six miles uphill, getting steeper and steeper. The first half is among the most stunning sections of this whole ride, as Loch Kishorn gives out to Skye, Rum and the distant peak of Resipole on Ardnamurchan in the back of beyond.

The huge buttress of Sgurr a' Chaorachain fills the sky to our right, and finally, inexorably, we are forced to round its base and head up into the great horseshoe below it. The road steepens. I am creeping now, just turning the gear over, as Phil manages to hold his rhythm from the lower slopes and presses on boldly. An ugly steel barrier protects us from a long tumble down to the meandering stream far below, like a silver shoelace on the valley floor. High above, straight in front, cars sparkle briefly as they crest the summit above a furious section of hairpins and zig-zags. No way. I'm never going to get up there. It turns out that the most difficult part is actually the mile up to the first hairpin.

Previous page: High above Loch Kishorn, the landing point for some of the country's finest seafood.

Left: The hairpins offer a little respite from the fierce gradients that precede them.

Below: The Bealach climbs 2,000ft in six miles, making it one of Britain's most respected climbs.

Even though the bends can reach 30 percent, the stretches between each corner offer a little respite. Before you can get to that corner though, you need to make it up that horrific last pitch of the main climb, where the gradient seems to relentlessly tilt the wrong way. Finally it eases, and I catch a glimpse of Phil on the stretch above me. When I finally struggle up to the top, he is waiting, grinning.

"Look at that." It is indeed some sight. Like a mini Scottish Stelvio, the road cascades in folding strips below us before plunging down to the distant loch. We just rode up that.

"What's the difference between full English and full Scottish?"

"Not sure if there's a distinct definition. Black pudding on the Scottish? They often have that potato scone thing, too."

"Do you remember Welsh Bloke? He used to go to the Clocktower Cafe in Isleworth, purely because he could order the special breakfast. No aggravation. Just special breakfast."

"How come?"

"When he was a young fellow in Swansea, he told me, he had to walk up a long hill to the café, repeating to himself, 'I'm going to have egg, two bacon, sausage, mushrooms, beans, grilled tomatoes, two slices of toast and a mug of tea. Egg, two bacon, sausage, mushrooms, beans, grilled tomatoes, two slices of toast and a mug of tea.'"

"So what happened?"

"He got in the door, they asked him what he wanted, and he just went, 'B-b-b-beans on toast.' He panicked."

"Contrary to popular belief, Tolkein didn't actually set Lord of the Rings in New Zealand."

"No?"

"Supposedly, the mines of Mordor where the orcs were created were Dudley and the Black Country."

"They haven't improved."

"The whole Mordor set up was obviously meant to invoke Germany in the 1930s."

"Obviously."

"But the mountains themselves... surely, he must have seen this view?"

Across the narrow strip of sea to the south, The Cuillins are like massive spikes, looking for all the world like a mystical drawing from one of Tolkein's books.

The descent into Applecross is simply the best fun you can have on a bike. Prolonged dry weather has swept the narrow band of grainy tarmac clear of loose gravel, encouraging the confident rider to attack the corners. The open mountainside allows you to see well in advance if anything is struggling up the pass towards you, which is lucky as there is barely room for the width of one family car. On a straight, four motorcyclists catch us, and two open their throttles to jet by before the next corner. I tuck even lower over the bars and pedal furiously for the remainder of the six-mile descent, leaving the other two bikers to follow me, and eventually get back on to the rear wheel of the mototourists at the cattle grid above the village. With a whoop, I shoot by. I will be first to the pub.

The water from the Applecross peaks rushes down to the sea through shady trees and deep peaty pools where salmon and trout lounge between brown mossy stones. The perfect place to cool off, I'd say. Bit Brokeback Mountain some might say, but it didn't cross my mind at the time. And to be honest, in water that cold, it's unlikely to cross your mind full stop.

The Bealach na Ba. You should come here, it truly is amazing. Just don't tell anybody about it, OK?

Right: Cooling off in a quiet pool of the Applecross River. The interior of the peninsula is completely uninhabited.

Next page: Raasay and Skye from Applecross. The Black Cuillins are regarded as some of the most challenging mountaineering targets in Europe.

August

Saturday Night, Sunday Morning

I'm flying down the Euston Road at 1am on Sunday morning, pitted tarmac slick with summer rain beneath the wheels. In my mind, it would be a time where things in the West End would be quietening down: showgoers packed into charabancs headed back to the provinces, drinkers supped up and safely on board last trains, clubbers queuing around Shoreditch pavements. Instead, the streets are rammed with folk headed who knows where, on foot, in taxis, on night buses, in the back of cycle rickshaws. Only two people, as far as I can see, are on bicycles. Fixed-wheel bicycles at that, one gear, one brake between them. That one brake is on the front of Phil's Condor; my Colnago relies entirely on me leaning back on the pedals to slow it down. Several oil tankers in the Persian Gulf have gone from full-steam-ahead to stationary in the time it has taken me to think about stopping to putting a foot on the kerb.

In the midst of this horror a siren is wailing. Not unusual for this time of night here, where the only immutables are the progress of emergency vehicles and an all-pervading vague scent of special cigarettes. When did Londoners start smoking pot at all available moments and why wasn't I informed?

The ambulance responsible for splitting the night is haring along the other carriageway in the opposite direction to us, past Euston Station, bound for the King's Cross end. As we approach the junction of Woburn Place, I realise with a fizz of pure terror that the ambulance is going to turn right, across our path. I hear Phil's one brake squeal as he tries to stop his fixie behind me, fighting the cyclist's perennial problem of trying to retain control when the front wheel stops going round while your back wheel is determined to press on.

Left: *Saturday night on Whitechapel Road in London's East End, deep in the heart of Ripper country.*

A brake. Luxury. There's nothing stopping 100kg of Deering (I'm including the bike in that, OK?) when he's grooving along on a fixed-wheel bike with similar properties to a giroscope in full flow. The flashing blue lights are like a strobe-light catching me in slow motion, the full beams of the ambulance's headlights illuminating me from point blank range. In a fraction of a second, my right leg will be crushed by the bumper.

My life does not flash before my eyes. Instead, I ponder on what happens when an ambulance runs somebody down. Do they stop or push on to their original destination? After all, the person in the back has been waiting longer. They could ring one of their mates to come out and see to me as they shoot off with bits of me stuck in their radiator.

Fortunately, ambulances are fitted with much more effective braking systems than these hopelessly inadequate but fashionable pieces of junk. I mouth a wide-eyed "sorry" to the enraged driver as I blow through the smoke left by his squealing brakes. Oops.

Below: The Shard, a *Blade Runner*-esque slice of architecture on London's skyline.

"That was a bit close."

"Can we have our real bikes back now?"

"My friend Marsha was rejected from being an ambulance driver for having too many speeding points on her licence."

"I thought that was the point?"

"Yes. That's pretty much what she said."

Let me take you back to those long winter nights when we were drinking mulled wine under the Christmas tree and talking about what we were going to do for this project.

"How about a London chapter?"

"Yeah, that would be good. Remember that night ride we did?"

"Oh yeah, up the Thames and back, that was a laugh. But it would be good to do something new."

"A circuit of the M25?"

"Wow. What a riveting read that would be."

"OK, OK… a tour of the Underground network."

"What, we're going to put planks between the rails and ride through the tunnels?"

"I've got it. What's quintessentially London? Full of places that everybody's heard of but most people have never been to?"

"Umm… Harry Potter?"

"No you idiot, real places."

"What? Hogwarts isn't real? Next you'll be claiming that quidditch isn't even in the Olympics."

"Stop talking and listen. Monopoly."

"You might be on to something."

"All the squares. In order."

"At night. Overnight between Saturday and Sunday."

"On fixies. Like the trendies. In jeans."

Left: *On a fixie, the interruptions caused by endless red lights are a real irritation.*

Next page: *The route visits every location on the Monopoly board. Can you spot them all?*

We're booting it back over Tower Bridge from Old Kent Road, headed for Whitechapel. I am rolling the gear over gingerly, acutely aware that should I need to stop quickly, I won't be able to. Simple as that. When we tip down the far side of the bridge, flying towards a long line of red brake lights, I can feel the bike running away underneath me and I try to push back on the pedals in the other direction to slow it down. I look like Stephen Hawking trying to avoid a flight of steps in a tailwind. Apparently, people actually choose to ride these things. I am in a permanent state of nearly soiling myself.

The discomfort in my nether regions is only enhanced by the wearing of jeans – the least cycling friendly item of clothing in the long and illustrious history of the bicycle. Those Edwardian women pedalling round Hyde Park in hooped dresses were more comfortable than me. They weren't likely to have their nether regions crushed into nut oil between saddle and gusset for starters.

"Denim. Cloth of kings."

"That's corduroy. Cord du rois."

"Ah. And hence I discover our first mistake."

"My nuts have gone either side of my old boy. It's like a division symbol down there."

"I'm not quite as bad. A percent sign, maybe."

"I'm going to buy Pall Mall and put a hotel on it. Just so I can run a hot bath and coax everything back into shape."

"I tell you what: pubs are open later these days, aren't they?"

"You're right. I don't know about you, but I find it intensely annoying that these bikes don't appear to have bottle cages."

"There's nothing for it. We'll simply have to make a stop. Just for refuelling purposes."

"Cheers."

"Your health."

By the time we hit the green squares of the West End, we've retraced our steps so many times we feel like commuters. That said, it hasn't taken long. We thought we'd have the city streets to ourselves, pedalling gently back west from Mayfair into the dawn and looking for a 24-hour café in Chelsea or Fulham for a spot of early breakfast. Instead, we find ourselves inhabiting a strangely opulent netherworld inhabited by lizard-like men in sports cars that cost more than my house and women clad almost exclusively in leopard skin.

"I bet she's got leopard skin socks on, too."

"Socks? I'll be amazed if she's not wearing leopard skin contact lenses. Have you ever seen the like?"

"How is it that the people with the most money have the least class?"

"You're just saying that to make yourself feel better about your tawdry existence."

"I do feel better. I don't want to be like them."

"I don't think they're chomping at the bit to trade places with you, Eddie Murphy. You can sleep easy in your entirely normal Ikea single bed tonight."

"Really? They speak very highly of you."

Opposite: *In 1968, an American called Robert P. McCulloch thought he was buying this piece of history but got it confused with the real London Bridge. This isn't true, but it's a fun myth anyway.*

Right: *Most pubs in the Square Mile are closed at the weekend, but not all of them, fortunately.*

You can't help wondering what Mr Waddington was thinking of when he was deciding which squares to put in. Legend has it that he planned it all out in an Islington pub called The Angel, which is how that made it in, despite not being a London street. With the myriad of interesting streets available between Piccadilly and Covent Garden, the selection of Vine Street is mystifying: it's nothing more than a dead-end yard a few paces deep. And as for Marlborough Street – there's no such road. We assumed that they meant Great Marlborough Street by Liberty's. That's where we head for, anyway.

"Do you know what's happening to me as I get older?"

"You're getting fatter and your hair is falling out?"

"No… well, yes, but that's not what I was thinking of. I get to the point where –"

"You look back upon your long years as an adult and speculate upon how little you've achieved?"

"Right, that's enough, I –"

"You resign yourself to never meeting a woman who will put up with your self-absorbed navel gazing for more than a fortnight?"

"You finished?"

"I think I've covered it. What is it?"

"Music. I've gone off it."

"Really? You used to live for music."

"I know. I couldn't give a hoot anymore. I went to see Mumford & Sons the other night."

"Oh yeah, they're alright though, right?"

"Rubbish. All their songs sounded exactly the same. Well, that's not quite true – they have two songs. The fast intense one and the anthemic one. I actually found myself thinking, 'I'm sure they've already done this one.'"

"And?"

"It was at that point that I realised I have become my Dad. Or anyone's dad."

Left: Cornering on a fixie is an exhilarating experience, but it takes a little getting used to.

"You're being way too harsh. Your Dad is much cooler than you."

"The other big disappointment was the line-up."

"In what way?"

"No sign of Fred Mumford anywhere. I was expecting a rhythm section of Timothy Claypole and Mrs Popov, with Mr and Mrs Meaker on backing vocals. Nothing."

"Perhaps they've all died."

"They ARE dead. *Rentaghost* would have been rubbish if they weren't."

"Rentaghost WAS rubbish."

"How dare you? All that talk about me being a hopeless, washed-up, middle-aged has-been is one thing, but to say *Rentaghost* was rubbish. You Philistine."

"Come on, I didn't say that about you. 'Has-been' suggests you were something once."

When we finally stretch out our legs in Berkeley Square to polish off our late night odyssey, it is finally a little quieter. The gentle pedal home down the Fulham Road beckons.

"Can you hear that?"

"Hear what?"

"I think I can hear a bird singing. A nightingale, probably."

"I find that about as likely as your tales of Richmond Park being full of parrots."

"It is! You don't know. Anyway, more amazing things have happened."

"Like what?"

"Well. There's a rumour that you're married. To a lady. As if."

Right: *It may not be the city that never sleeps, but London certainly stays busy late into the night.*

Next page: *Honestly, it's like Piccadilly Circus round here sometimes.*

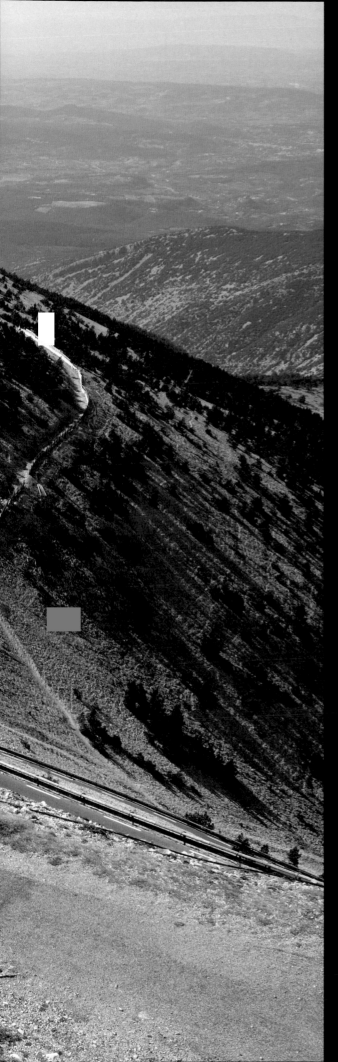

September

Mont Ventoux

In July, on my way back from the preposterously beautiful slopes of the Bealach na Ba, I had stopped off in Edinburgh to catch up with an old friend, John Anderson of Renner cycle clothing. We drank too many coffees and talked about the rides Phil and I had already done and the ones to come for the remaining five months in the saddle.

"So you're going to Ventoux, then?" Anderson asked me.

"Yep," I replied, "That's the plan."

"OK… take this with you," he said, handing me a black and white Renner cycling cap.

"Thanks. What for?" I frowned.

"You'll know when the time comes."

A couple of months later, we're in Avignon. As we cross the square under the golden gaze of Our Lady perched upon the highest point of the Pope's fourteenth-century place of exile, Phil and I see one of the more bizarre sights of this long and interesting year. A lady is carrying a cat. And the cat is wearing a jumper. To be more accurate, the cat is wearing a custom knitted pink hoody, paws poking out ludicrously through the arm holes and the hood raised and pointy on its little head. To give the tabby credit, it has an expression on its face that lets us know that it is fully aware of how absolutely stupid it looks. I am caught in a triangle between compassion in the face of animal cruelty, pure hilarity, and sympathy for the pet's visibly acute shame.

Left: The barren, lunar landscape at the summit of Mont Ventoux is often mistaken for snow from a distance.

It gets worse as she unfurls a lead – you heard me right – and attempts to "walk" the aggrieved moggy like some kind of twisted Barbara Woodhouse. You'll be pleased to hear that Puss-in-Hood is having absolutely none of it.

The narrow streets of Avignon curve and dip their way around the old *grandes maisons* and *hôtels de ville* that cosy up to the Palais des Papes, which has dominated the old Comtat since the Pope fled Rome for here eight centuries ago. Much has changed since then, but not everything. Their ancient residence is still imposing and wonder-inspiring, even if that old bridge doesn't make it across the river anymore. Must be the millions of dancing feet over the ages.

One thing that definitely hasn't changed is the wind. As we roll around those medieval walls looking for the Carpentras road out of town, the Mistral whips around the corners, even this early in the morning. It's a warm blast, racing along the Rhône and messing up the neatest of Provençal streets by picking up yesterday's

neatly stacked rubbish from outside the cafes and shops and dispersing it around the town. You'd think they'd know that was going to happen, wouldn't you?

"Breezy."
"Hmm. Not cold, though."

Ventoux, where we're headed on this beautifully bright September morning, means the windy mountain. Depending on who you listen to, anyway. With winds reaching 60mph for 240 days a year (I know!), I'm inclined to agree with that reading. At 1,912m above sea level, the summit is nowhere near the heights of the Alpine monsters like the Galibier or the Col d'Agnello, or the Pyrenean passes of the Tourmalet or the Aubisque. What makes Ventoux different, however, is its splendid isolation. Those other climbs sit surrounded by the massifs of some of Europe's most significant mountains, whereas the "Giant of Provence" towers over the vineyards of the Côtes du Rhône far below.

Below: Cats on leads. Unacceptable everywhere, except Avignon it seems.

Below right: The Palais des Papes has kept watch over the Rhône Valley and the Comtat since the fourteenth century.

Opposite: The road up Mont Ventoux winds through the vignobles and the Forêt de Rolland, then out onto the bleached heights.

Below: *The village of Bedoin, at the foot of the Giant of Provence, enjoys its place in cycling lore.*

Our start point in Avignon, on the banks of the Rhône not far from where it begins to fan out lazily on its final approach to the Med, is squarely at sea level so we'll have to cover every centimetre of those 1,912m if we're going to conquer it.

Ventoux is a famous mountain for many reasons: that unique solitariness, the Ventoux reds so popular across France as staple *vins-de-table*, the desert of white that crowns its proud summit. But Ventoux's place in the public consciousness was earned by cycling and, specifically, the Tour de France.

On 13 July 1967, I was one week old. Phil was nine months. It's fair to say that neither of us remembers that much about that day, but our later lives have had reason to recall that date on more than a few occasions. England's finest cyclist before a certain Mr Wiggins came along, Tom Simpson, was bidding to be the first Briton to win the world's greatest race. He'd tasted success before, becoming World Road Race Champion and winning the Tour of Flanders, and had proved a worthy enough Tour contender to have worn the yellow jersey before.

On that day, as well as facing what many classed as the hardest mountain in cycling thanks to its relentless slopes and fearsome heat, Tom was facing an uphill battle to stay in the race for the yellow jersey, which was threatening to move beyond his reach on the shoulders of Maitres Jacques, Jacques Anquetil, the first five-time winner of the Tour. As he moved out of the forest that shadows most of the climb and on to the bare rock surrounding the summit, Tom was clearly in discomfort and unable to match the attacks moving off the front of the race. His reputation was built on extreme willpower and strength in the face of adversity and this day was no exception as he ground onwards, ignoring the gradient and length of the climb, the searing heat and his own lack of energy.

As he moved closer to the summit and the thinner air, he wavered for a moment, clearly struggling against his circumstances. Then he wobbled and fell.

Instantly, his team car crunched to a halt and he was attended by his friend and mechanic, Harry Hall. Though clearly in distress, Tom was desperate to continue, perhaps still believing he could limit his losses to Anquetil and the others and still have a chance in the '67 race. "Put me back on my bike," he is reputed to have whispered to Hall, and his trusty old mate did exactly that, pushing him off again, within sight of the huge Thunderbird 3-like tower on top of the mountain. Tom rode a little way, then collapsed again, never to continue. He died.

An autopsy showed traces of amphetamines and brandy in his system, but to think of Tom Simpson as a drug cheat in a time where there was scant control of such things, misses the point. Tom Simpson died because his will to succeed exceeded his body's abilities to carry him. He remains a hero to everybody who has ever ridden up a hill and thought, "I'm going to have to stop in a minute."

That stage began down on the coast in Marseille and continued over the summit and down to Carpentras, the old Roman town nearest the western foot of the mountain. In more recent times, to promote more attacking racing, the finish line has been drawn slap bang on the crest of the summit outside that strange tower block with the red and white aerial on top. Clearly visible from the plains way, way below, it looks like a little obelisk, perhaps a memorial to some local landowner or war hero from the misty past. It gives the tourist a sense of the mountain's size to realise that the little pointy thing on its peak is in fact the best part of 150ft high and would sit happily alongside the architecture of Westbourne Park or Whalley Range.

We've begun in Avignon to make this ride a beautiful, tough, but doable tour of the famous mountain. Tweaked to take in these dreamy vignoble lanes that lead us away from the Rhône, it runs out at about 100 miles.

We're riding for an hour and a half or so through the vineyards of ripe black grapes awaiting the tender hands that will lay them carefully into comfortable little trays any day now.

"They call themselves winegrowers, but they're not are they?"

"What do you mean?"

They're winemakers. They're grapegrowers. You can't grow wine any more than you can mine jewellery."

Tractors chugging happily along with big plastic vats of grapes in tow pass us on the road, and we see pickers carefully laying bunches in trays. It's not like the grab-it-quick fruit picking you see in the Vale of Evesham or Kentish orchards.

"These are all black grapes, so they must be making red wine."

"Aha! The colour of the wine isn't necessarily dependent on the colour of the grape. Red wine is made when they leave the black skins on and pulp the lot. But the juice from a black grape is green so you can make white wine from it."

"Wow, I never knew that."

"See. You don't know everything after all. You'll be hoping that comes up on University Challenge now, won't you?"

We reach the consummately Provençal village of Bedoin that nestles under the southern slopes of the Giant, surrounded by vines heavy with black juicy grapes. Bikes are everywhere. You'd assume that there was an event on; it's like the start of some big sportive event, but no: this is the daily business of Bedoin. We stop at the famous old fountain where Tour riders of yore paused to refill their bottles with crystal clear water that has filtered down the slopes of the village's dominant overlord, Ventoux. Bedoin bidons. Unlike those heroes, we find time for a coffee too. I strongly consider the option of fortifying it with brandy and amphetamines, but reason that ultimately that didn't help Tom. And ordering them may cause problems.

Some pigeons drop down nervously from the plane tree branches above to sip the water in the trough below the fountain. I catch a flash of white and orange out of the corner of my eye, and a scrawny cat flies out of the nearby bushes like a swooping sparrowhawk. There's a puff of plumage and the birds are airborne, the cat clutching at their tail feathers to no avail. Cursing in cat language, the defeated feline stalks off.

Phil – That's two irritated cats in the space of a few hours. I remember my family cat, Frankie, coming home once when I was a teenager. She jumped up on the garden fence proudly holding a massive wood pigeon in her jaws, at least the same size as her. As she jumped down onto the lawn with it, she bumped into the ground and lost her grip for a fraction of a second and the pigeon flew out of her mouth, like a cricket ball popping out of a fielder's hand at the moment of impact after he's made a magnificent, diving effort to catch it. I can still hear the wail she let out. Long and anguished. She couldn't have sounded more bereft if she'd realised she'd forgotten to buy a lottery ticket on the week her numbers came up. Cats do irritated very well.

Opposite top: *Picking the Ventoux grapes is a painstaking activity and needs much care.*

Opposite bottom: *Choosing the right moment to remove the fruit from the vine is crucial.*

Right: *Walking in the footsteps of legends at the fountain in the village of Bedoin.*

A line just past the fountain tells us we are at Kilometre Zero. Another 22 to the top. The first few gently skirt the base from west to east. When the road doubles back under the trees and begins to ride the banks of a gully into the heart of the mountain, I know immediately that I'm going to be in trouble. Phil starts to pull away and I concentrate on my own rhythm rather than killing myself to match him. He's carrying his smaller camera so I know I'll be seeing him again and steel myself against not looking too wrecked for the inevitable Deering-struggling-up-mountain shots.

I'm in my lowest gear and having difficulty staying on top of it. I've often wondered why Ventoux is rated as so hard by those who know about these things, despite the statistics not stacking up too harshly. I'm finding out right now. It's the mountain's relentless nature, not the overall gradient, or length, or the wind, or the heat. These elements come together to punish the rider, although we're avoiding the worst of that July heat and enjoying a prettier landscape by tackling it at harvest time.

In the UK we measure the gradient of our hills by the steepest part: Porlock Hill, for instance, runs out at 1-in-4 or 25 percent. In France, with longer climbs the norm, they opt for the average gradient per kilometre. Experience has shown me that anything over nine percent in the mountains is really, really hard. Pretty much the whole 10km under the Forêt de Rolland averages out around ten percent. This is a fact that is pretty unpalatable in itself, but not that unusual in European mountain riding. What is pretty unique, is that there are next to no bends, no hairpins, no let off. This isn't a carefully constructed old drovers' road

Right: *The hardest part of Mont Ventoux is not the famed white summit but the incessant brutal gradient through the forest.*

contouring round the slopes, it's a full-on push for glory at an unadulterated, unabridged, obnoxious, offensive, in-your-face rate that will find you out. And I've been found out.

I target the yellow-and-white milestones ticking off the kilometres. No stop or rest or stretch of the spine is allowed unless it is at one of these silent sentinels that have impassively recorded the passage of thousands of cyclists across generations. I stop at 12, 11 and 10, stretching my vertebrae and drinking deep of the Bedoin fountain water. Number nine comes and goes, then so does eight, both without the need for a pause, and now I start to believe.

Phil is waiting on a bend where we can glimpse the summit through the trees. The sunshine is hot, but the rapidly increasing wind is cool, blowing in off the central Alps who cast their brother Ventoux out into his lonely situation some millennia previously.

"You OK?"
He gets a nod, but no words.

We press on silently until we breach the tree line and the road flattens ever so slightly. Ahead of us, cyclists, motorcyclists and motorists wander around their respective modes of transport outside Chalet Reynard, one of those strange isolated mountain *relais* so beloved of the French, and the only real sign of civilisation between the start of the forest and the summit.

We refill our bidons from an ancient pump and guzzle down a litre or two of naturally chilled, sweet water.

"Easier from here, apparently."
"Yep, and that wind is behind. Mainly."
"Ready?"
"Don't wait for me."

I hang my helmet over my bars, too hot to wear it. The next kilometre is indeed easier as I'm blown up the shallower gradient by a fierce gale. In the nature of mountain winds though, the direction and force of the breeze are capricious, and a corner nearly brings me to a shuddering standstill. The brightness of the rock all around glitters through the thinning atmosphere as we climb higher and higher and I regret my choice of yellow lenses today. The darker the better up here. At least the wind means that glasses will never steam up.

I've never seen anything quite like this. The bleached stones, often mistaken for snow from the bottom, glare back at you, while, far, far below, it seems as though all of France is laid out like a giant road atlas. It's more like satellite photography than a diorama. The sky at this altitude is a silly sort of blue, so deep, so all-encompassing that it appears completely surreal. That's something else I'd forgotten about: altitude. The thinning of the air, the slow drain of oxygen, has always had a bad effect on me.

Left: *The road through the forest is protected from the fierce wind that visits the open upper slopes.*

It's not so much breathlessness, just a real drain on the muscles. I get it above 1,500m, so I'm getting it now. The 1,912m we're covering today will easily mark the highest point of this book and I'm grateful for avoiding anything higher.

The highest pass in the Alps is the Col de l'Iseran, which tops out at a dizzying height of 2,270m. By my reckoning, if I tried to ride the Iseran, I'd be progressively struggling to get more oxygen in before I'd even really started. Don't expect to see *12 Months in the High Alps* in your local bookshop any time soon. The worst thing to do when climbing at an insistent speed on a high pass is to take a drink from your bidon. The one or two breaths of air that you missed while gulping some energising fluid take an aeon to replace and a rider can find himself gasping like a goldfish after escaping the bowl.

Professional cyclists have long known the benefits of training at altitude to prepare yourself for those days. Physiologically, this increases the number of red blood cells in your bloodstream, increasing the amount of oxygen your blood can carry. This is also the benefit of taking the illegal performance-enhancing drug that has done such harm to cycling's reputation, EPO. Before there was a reliable test for EPO, many cyclists bought apartments in the Sierra Nevada or the Dolomites to claim that their improved performance was natural.

Below: What looks like a small obelisk from the plains below turns out to be a 150ft tall tower block.

A few yards after the memorial the road meets the Col de Tempêtes, the first point where a view to the north and east is afforded via a windy gap. As Phil leaves his bike for a moment to take a picture, the Windy Mountain takes a little something back from him: the gale literally picks his bike up off of its two wheels and smacks it into the stones. His curses are ripped from his mouth by the wind, broken into individual letters and scattered into the distant west, eventually landing shattered somewhere in the Languedoc or Midi.

I can't match his fury-fired pace up the last steep pitch to the summit, and I crawl up to the last corner some minutes after him. I don't think I can make it round the steep hairpin that guards the finish line, but I hear his shouts of encouragement and see the camera raised. That does it. One last push and I'm there.

The glory of achievement. We would love to savour it, but this wind is ripping us to shreds. And there's a 22km descent to come.

Off the brakes for as long as possible, soft tyres clutching at the grippy surface as we lean these machines over at improbable angles, we descend. Never mind Lance Armstrong, I feel like I could beat Frankel or Ayrton Senna down here. Whooping with spontaneous delight, we point our bars at Malaucene at 60mph, all the pain of the ascent forgotten. We did it.

Above: *Descending Mont Ventoux is like getting on to a roller coaster and being told that you're driving.*

Right: *The timeless pull of Provence for cyclists is easy to appreciate.*

Next page: *The Giant of Provence rises up from the Rhône Valley at dawn.*

October

L'Eroica

Once upon a time, a man named Bob Johnson invited me to a bike jumble. It was on a Saturday afternoon down near Woking in Surrey. Chelsea and Brentford must have both been playing away. There must have been nothing on at the cinema. I must have just finished reading a book and yet to start a new one. I know these things, because I went to the bike jumble.

It was in a school car park. Men of indeterminate age stood behind formica tables with vaguely defensive looks on their faces. In front of them, their wares were spread. These strange items ranged from a crusty old leather racing helmet that looked like it had been dug up at Sutton Hoo, to a bent rusty wheel of use to nobody but an avant garde record producer looking for something to bang with a stick.

But Bob was loving it. These were his people. He moved among them like an alcoholic going from pub to pub in an old market town. He'd pick up a toe strap here, a cable ferrule there.

"Look at this," he said, gingerly picking up a rusty chain with the wrong end of a biro.

"Hmm. I can see immediately what you could do with that," I frowned.

"Yes?"

"Throw it away. You know, like a normal person would."

Left: The Castello di Brolio welcomes weary returnees on l'Eroica.

So here we are in 2012 in Bob's workshop. Suddenly this arcane world of adjustable headsets, screw-on blocks and Campag delta brakes appears esoteric and beautiful. And important. Phil and I are on our way to Tuscany and l'Eroica, the perfect way for any cyclist to end the European summer. Tuscany and, more specifically, Chianti is a sought-out destination at any time of year, but when the leaves are beginning to turn and the shadows lengthen it really is God's country. If we were going at another time of year, we'd be polishing carbon wheels and trimming 10-speed cassettes, but l'Eroica is different to other challenges. That's because if you want to ride l'Eroica, you'll have to do it on an old bike. More specifically, according to the official communication:

"Only the following will be accepted: road racing bikes built before 1987, with switch gear lever on the down tube, toe clips and straps, external brake cables on handlebars – no quick release pedals – ALL THESE FEATURES ARE OBLIGATORY!"

Crikey, alright, calm down, old bikes, we get it. We know we'll be OK. We know Bob.

We fly into Pisa and retrieve our bike boxes. In these, for which we were coerced into adding an usurious amount of extra cash by British Airways, the World's Favourite Airline, are two rather beautiful old bicycles. Phil's steed for the weekend is a blue Pogliaghi from 1975, painstakingly equipped with contemporary yellow accessories. Mine is a champagne-coloured 1976 Chesini of rare class. We're excited, but before we can get them out of their coffins, we have to negotiate an hour or two of Italian roads and, more pertinently, Italian driving. With two lanes for each carriageway and concrete walls where one might hope for a hard shoulder or a central reservation, the autostrada is not full of laughs.

Right: *Chianti's thickly wooded hills can melt the heart of the most jaded traveller.*

The guy doing 160 klicks flashing his lights behind you is one thing, the old feller doing 30 in the inside lane is something else.

L'Eroica is centred on the gorgeous old town of Gaiole-in-Chianti, sat prettily in the lap of the surrounding wooded hillsides. We've driven here on Saturday morning from our lovely accommodation in Radda-in-Chianti, another bastide-type village a handful of kilometres to the west of here. We're in town a day early for the event in order to experience the world's greatest bike jumble.

Bob is here too and he's trembling. Salivating. Once again, there are formica tables, but this marketplace is teeming with wonder in stark contrast to that school car park. Italian voices chatter around displays featuring thousands of old silver hubs, hundreds of multi-coloured woollen jerseys, and dozens of enamel head badges. Euros are changing hands faster than you can say Campag Super Record rear mech.

We're here with Ian and Jared from La Fuga. They're both ex-racers – Ian rode full-time for a team in Tuscany – and now they run holidays for people who want to experience the lifestyle. We wanted to see what it was like to do one of these trips and have tagged on to their l'Eroica bunch. Right now, they're haggling with a man in overalls in Italian about purchasing a vintage bike so Jared can ride the *strade bianche* with the rest of us tomorrow. There's a suspicion that anything on sale in Gaiole carries an Eroica premium on the price, but needs must, and this is the biggest collection of immaculate vintage bikes that you'll find anywhere in the world. Eventually, Ian's knowledge of the local ways strikes them a deal, and the tall Canadian beams next to his new ride.

We've been given our numbers and instructions, typically packaged Eroica-style in a neat vintage cotton musette. I'm in the high 5000s, Phil, improbably, is a cool number 17.

Below: Gaiole's l'Eroica market is a mecca for vintage collectors.

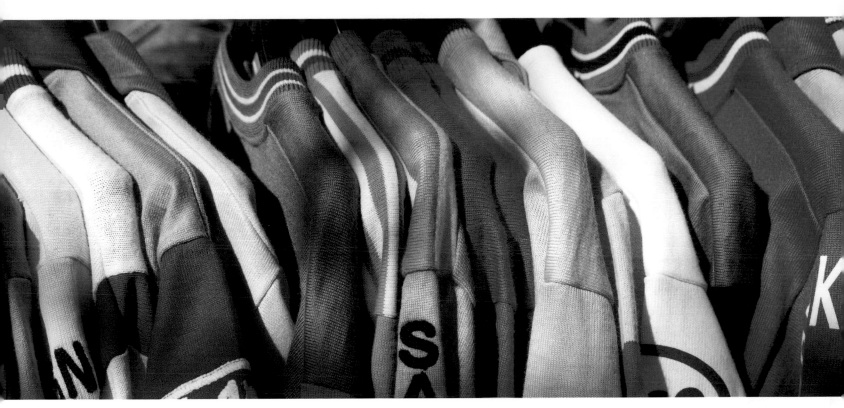

He is extremely pleased with himself until Ian starts to chuckle knowingly.

"What?"

"Google 'Italian 17,'" he suggests.

I fiddle with my iPhone. "Ooooh, Phil. You've got the number of death."

"Eh? What are you talking about?"

"Heptadecaphobia, my friend. Fear of the unlucky number 17. It's an anagram of 'I am dead' in Roman numerals. Or something like that. No wonder that one was left over."

"That's just great."

I see a guy ride past on a Dave Russell and my mind drifts off... I started riding a bike as an 80s teenager with a guy called Doug Thomson. I had a Raleigh that had been sprayed into a Benotto to hide its dubious provenance, Doug had saved up for a Dave Russell from the Berkshire frame builder around the same time. Together we explored long miles of Berkshire, Buckinghamshire and Oxfordshire road, loving

Top: Wool was the cycling fabric of choice for generations. Beware of putting too much in your pockets – your jersey will stretch down to your knees.

Above: Whatever you need for your old bike, you'll find it here.

our new sport. Eventually I moved back to London, Doug went off to uni, and in those dark days before Facebook, we lost touch.

"John Deering," says the man on the Dave Russell. "Doug Thomson. How have you been?" The magic that crackles in the air around Gaiole is certainly working.

It's 6am on Sunday morning. We've rolled out of Gaiole in the dark, along a winding valley overhung with thick foliage, then swung left and climbed up to the foot of the imposing Castello Di Brolio, looming out of the pre-dawn sky. We've come here this early because we want to see one of the most memorable aspects of l'Eroica. This point marks the start of the first stretch of *strada bianca*, the unsurfaced chalk roads that give the route its unique character. Through a series of little hairpins, the white road zig-zags up under a yew forest to the castle walls on top of the hill. What makes this particularly special is that somebody got up even earlier than us and lit candles along the roadside to show us our way. Pausing at the top, the only sound below is a crackling like a camp fire as ancient rubber crunches over the loose gravel.

Every now and then a voice rings out and a group of enthusiastic men in matching wool jerseys from a forgotten age come out of the trees. It seems obligatory that each of these groups features one jolly jackanapes who insists on babbling at high volume at all times, the intention being to raise a smile from his suffering companions. It's not an approach that meets universal approval, but nobody punches him, which after a time I find surprising.

Top left: *Bikes are kept true to their heritage with the utmost attention to detail.*

Left: *Preparing for an event in 2012, not 1955, as it may appear.*

Opposite: *Climbing the* strada bianca *by candlelight. Early starters leave at 5.30am, when it's still dark.*

We shoot down the rough far side of the castle's ramparts, hearts in mouths at the lack of control we can impart on to the loose surface. Jared's words of advice come back to me from our pre-event briefing.

"Just remember: milking the cow. Milking the cow," he told us, miming the action of pulling udders. The point is to get your hands right into the bends of your bars, enabling your arms to soak up the bumps. It's good to get on the drops, to get low, to keep your centre of gravity down, to spread your weight along the frame and stay as safe as possible on the corners. But if you grip the ends of the bars, the part horizontal to the ground, you'll be shuddering over the rough roads. Get your hands up in those hooks like a boxer taking guard and the stuttering effect is significantly reduced.

I'm just getting the hang of this when there is a resounding crack and my front tyre loses every PSI of air in a nanosecond. Gah. I had been in favour of fitting stronger tyres for the event, but Bob's insistence on staying contemporary to the 70s set-up meant a silky Italian amber-walled number that was now wearing a gash that Zorro would have been proud of. Jared screeches to a halt when he sees me struggling through the snapping of my first tyre lever and brings Canada's most powerful thumbs to bear on my complaining rubber. This is why event support is good.

The roads in Tuscany are marvellous feats of engineering. There are virtually no flat bits whatsoever, but there is also an almost complete absence of super-steep gradients. The roads follow the contours around every combe, climb gently out of every valley, and descend carefully back into the next.

Left: Carbon fibre, lycra and hard-shell helmets would all look ridiculous here.

173

As we approach the medieval towers of Siena, the countryside opens up around us. Instead of the forested and castellated hilltops, we find ourselves trundling through beautiful rolling farmland. Replacing the tightly packed terraces of olives and vines, long columns of cypresses and freshly ploughed chalky fields line our route.

"We've seen our fair share of grapes this year, eh? Vineyards look the same wherever we've been, but the olives look different, some of the trees grow on little flat ledges.

"Do you know why they plant them on terraces?"

"Well, I'm guessing that they grow them on hillsides because of the drainage; they don't want sodden soil. Is it to do with that?"

"That's not the reason for the terracing. They pick the olives by putting nets under the trees and giving them a good old shake when they're ready to drop. If they're not ripe, they don't fall. And the terraces…"

"If the trees weren't on terraces, the olives would all roll off. Lost to the bottom of the hill?"

"Bingo."

"Mmm, sounds very dubious to me."

There is a surreal peacefulness around us. The morning is wearing on, and fortunately it's not as hot as yesterday, otherwise this would be a real slog. All around us, men are wearing clothes that were fabricated at some time in the second half of the last century. The occasional rider who decides to tackle the route clad in his modern lycra and hardshell helmet looks incongruous. For most of us, the overriding feeling is of being an actor in a film. Facial hair is all around us in a variety of forms, each display a little more outlandish than the last. I wonder if the men sprouting these creations are genuinely cool, as they appear to be to me, or whether it's just the Eroica effect, and they would look like idiots strolling round Westfield. There is a steampunk slant on the whole event, like being in a two-wheeled Jules Verne novel. I expect Captain Nemo to overtake us in a bizarre pedal-powered dirigible at any moment.

Above: *It's not all castles and vistas. There's still hard graft to be done in the fields.*

Right: *It's not just the bicycles that are prehistoric, but the road surfaces, too.*

We've plumped for the 135km version of this event, believing it to be not too difficult. We were wrong. Most of the people we've spoken to over the weekend are doing the 78km route, which appeared little more than a morning jaunt on a map, but in hindsight represents a significant investment of time and effort. The lack of flat roads and the constant interruption of unsurfaced sections exacts a huge toll on pretty but basic bicycles and their unprepared riders. For a start, the spread of gears on a 70s bike covers approximately half the range of that on a twenty-first century machine. The amount of power one can generate through an old steel frame dissipates like water through a fist, although there is no disputing the smoothness of the ride. Getting out of the saddle and blasting up a hill is a chancy enterprise, with the lack of gears, the lack of power and the loose chalky gravel combining to thwart most efforts. The only alternative is the slow, hard grunt. When this starts to happen every few minutes, the rider's body, already battered by the juddering descents, begins to complain insistently. It's really hard.

My saddle has slipped upwards, the nose pointing upward at about 30 degrees above the horizontal. My crotch is acutely aware of this change in position. In answer to its high-pitched yelps, I hop off and pull out my allen keys to adjust it, only to find that I need a spanner.

"A spanner? For God's sake, who uses a spanner on a bike in this day and age?"

"True, but we're not in this day and age, are we?"

Left: "Let's come back here again on our real bikes."

We push on, the recalcitrant saddle resistant to all attempts to right it. It is stuck faster than it was in its correct position. Bumping around on the *strada bianca* as we approach yet another climb, I yank at the gear lever to look for a little respite and manage to pull it all the way round without shifting the chain out of the smallest cog.

"Great."

"Looks like you've pulled the cable through."

"I'd better stop and fix it."

"Yeah. You've got a 9mm spanner with you, have you?"

"Oh, for God's sake!"

We are at the furthest possible southerly point on our route when I have my second puncture. We're headed back towards Siena when I have the third. And we're scaling one of the day's roughest ridge roads when I have the fourth. That will be all my inner tubes used up, then. Phil has one left, and offers it to me like the pal he is.

"I don't think that's a good idea."

"Why not?"

"If you have a puncture, we're both stuffed."

"Hmmm."

"You go on. This is why we have support, for moments like this. The La Fuga AA."

"OK. See you later. Just one thing…"

"Yeah?"

"Number 17 not looking so unlucky now, is it?"

1970s bike, woollen jersey, wooden-soled shoes, embroidered shorts, cotton cap… 2012 iPhone.

Above: *Punctures punctuate l'Eroica. By the following morning, every road sign will have a flat tyre draped over it.*

Opposite: *Walking holidays are also popular in Tuscany.*

Ian can't, however, get the La Fuga van up to me, as the event bars him from the *strade bianche*. He will position himself at the far end of the section I'm on and wait for me there. Neither of us know that this is five miles away. Five miles. Of stony track. In thin, wooden-soled shoes. There has been far too much crassness amongst these sordid pages already, so I will spare your eyes. Just.

Meanwhile, Phlash is having a feast.

Phil – I left old Captain Oates trudging along his lonely farrow at his insistence and headed north. After the briefest of chats with Ian in the mercy wagon, which was an amusingly long distance from where I'd left the poor wounded soldier, I reached the second feed station. My word. We've been to a few feed stations over the course of this book, downing bananas, honey sandwiches and protein bars from Ronse to the Rhondda, but none have been quite like this. There are sweet things, of course, but they range from freshly cut Montelimar nougat in original rice paper, to neatly sliced tranches of fresh bread spread with jam to deliciously moist pieces of fruit cake. There is more, though. There is a most tasty wild boar stew. And, even more incredibly, there is wine. Chianti Classico, naturally. To be honest, it's easy for a man to overdo it all slightly, especially after 100km of sapping unsurfaced Tuscan roadway. What I am blissfully unaware of as I tuck into a second portion of cinghiale casseruola – *don't mind if I do, thank you very much – is that I am about to scale the biggest hill of the ride.*

All the way up the next hour or so of back-breaking loose chalk hillside, my churning stomach put one thought and one thought only into my mind… couldn't they have put that feed station at the top?

An Englishman's home may well be his castle, but an Italian's home is invariably a castle on

top of a hill. No hilltop is missing one. As we wind back out of the long rolling vistas south of Siena towards Gaiole, the hills and trees close in around us again. Ways round the hills being harder to come by as the little mountains begin to proliferate, there is a merciful decrease in the number of unsurfaced sections, and our aching gussets get a well-earned rest. Those of us without a saddle pointing towards the heavens do, anyway.

The atmosphere that greets the returning warriors in Gaiole is something to behold. These men – there are very few women to be spotted on l'Eroica, possibly because it attracts the type of stuff-loving nerd that you find so rarely amongst the infinitely more sensible female of the species – have dragged their

twentieth-century kit around the countryside for many hours and are grateful to be back. They take cold Birra Morettis from the fridges and lie on the grass. Some smile, some grimace. Some lovingly wipe the white film from their old machines. Some hurl their bikes to the turf in frustration. Me, I rest the Chesini carefully against a wall with a weary smile, recognizing that I've been allowed a glimpse of old class, and resolve to come back again and ride these amazing roads on my real bike.

"You missed it. The greatest feed station in the history of cycling."

"So you said. Wine, *cinghiale*, nougat… was it Chianti?"

"The world famous Chianti Classico."

Opposite top left: Cinghiale *and Chianti Classico provide the most civilised of all race refreshments.*

Opposite left: *It would pay to just put on some vintage clothing and hang around the feed stops for a free meal.*

Above: *Traction is hard to come by on loose surfaces on old bikes. Walking works, too.*

Above, all pictures:
L'Eroica encourages entrants to immerse themselves in the heritage of the sport.

"That is genuinely world famous. Unlike some other things."

"What do you mean?"

"Oh, nothing really, just something I was daydreaming about during my five mile yomp earlier today."

"Go on?"

"Well, the phrase 'world famous' surely means renowned throughout the globe, right?"

"I would agree. Like Chianti Classico."

"Yes, you could go into a bar in Oregon, say, and ask for a glass of Chianti and they would know what you're talking about. However, I don't think that if I was, say, walking the *barrios* of Rio de Janeiro that it was likely that a local would say to me, 'Oh wow, you're English, I would love to see the Pump Room Café in Brighton one day.'"

"I take it there is a self-proclaimed 'World Famous Pump Room Café' in Brighton?"

"Yes. Likewise, the chances of a Siberian lobster fisherman asking me to bring him a plate of the Rose & Crown's world famous sausages next time I visit are slim."

"There's a 'World Famous Frankenstein Pub' in Edinburgh."

"Really? That's weird."

"Why?"

"I haven't heard of it."

Late on Sunday night, riding done for the day, Phil, Doug and I plough manfully through the biggest pizza known to man. We're outside a little trattoria on a corner of the main road in Radda. In the dark, single white lights occasionally wind their way slowly up the hill and past the restaurant, eight kilometres still separating them from Gaiole and the blessed relief of the finish line. These men are finishing the epic 200km version of l'Eroica, which follows the ridge route through Radda on its last stretch. By definition, if they are on the long route then they must have started before 7am this morning. They have been out there for maybe 13 or 14 hours today, struggling against the incessant hills, the unforgiving *strade bianche* and their ancient bicycles from before dawn until after dark.

Spontaneously, people stand in the restaurant and applaud these silent pilgrims. We know bravery when we see it. L'Eroica does indeed have a few heroes.

Next page: *There always seems to be time to take in your surroundings on l'Eroica.*

November

Exmoor Beast

Growing up in the 1950s, my Dad was obsessed with Exmoor. Post-war Fulham would occasionally be swapped for long family train and bus journeys heading ever westwards through Middlesex, Berkshire and Wiltshire before the red soil of Somerset began to appear in the fields and the brooding heather heights of Dunkery filled the horizon. He read and re-read the tales of crazy Victorian priests charging across the moor from Stoke Pero, poor travellers being pixy-led into spending long nights on the wind-blasted Chains, and of gargantuan men pushing lifeboats over the moors to save stranded sailors.

More than anything else, he read Blackmore's Lorna Doone, the characters coming to life against the backdrop of the real places in which the melodrama takes place. The amiable giant John Ridd, the beautiful and mysterious Lorna herself, shot in Oare Church on her wedding day, and his favourite, that heartless ogre, a baddie straight out of the Western films Dad loves, Carver Doone. It was Carver that shot Lorna in jealous rage at her marriage to John, but who was sucked to a grisly doom in one of the great mires that perennially trap the unwary on the moor.

Dad was probably reading Lorna Doone again when he took Mum on honeymoon to Exmoor in a borrowed car in 1966 while England won the World Cup back in London. He was certainly still reading it when we returned there as a family many times; pointing out to my brother Rob and me the spot on Badgworthy Water where John saw Lorna for the first time, telling us that the long-abandoned houses we were scrambling over with Action Men was where the Doones had conducted their long reign of terror from, like an eighteenth-century Corleone family.

Left: The wide expanse of Dunkery, the highest part of Exmoor Forest.

As a 10-year old boy, Dad had been playing in the garden of a place he was staying at with Nanny Deering, Grandad Deering and Auntie Ann. A solitary sort of boy, he'd apparently found a way of being both bowler and batsman simultaneously as long as there was a wall to return the ball from the bowler's hand on to the bat. It was in this manner that he lost a tennis ball in the shrubbery behind St Petrock's Church in Porlock. Despite seeing exactly where it ended up, he just couldn't find it, and spent much of the holiday searching for it. Years later, Rob and I would be despatched to comb the same spot, just in case we could retrieve what he couldn't.

Exmoor to me has long been the place to come in the autumn. Though we often used to come here in August during school holidays, it was our autumn half term trips that I remember best. We were probably a little bit older then, and allowed to venture out for walks without our parents, all the way along the tumbling, gushing East Lyn from Brendon to Lynmouth or even the Valley of Rocks, slippery autumn leaves and blackened burnt bracken under every step. Later, it was my first holiday under my own steam as my girlfriend and I brought our state-of-the-art 1980s steel Muddy Fox mountain bikes along the same paths in another rain-sodden Exmoor November.

So when we were looking for an autumnal destination for *12 Months in the Saddle*, it was the first place I thought of, and Phil was more than happy to explore a bit more of the West Country.

Above: *Exmoor girls. Sheep are constant companions on rides in Britain and Ireland.*

Opposite: *Fording East Water below Cloutsham. You are never far from water in this part of the world.*

It's probably not entirely coincidental that this also happens to be the setting for Britain's finest autumn sportive, the challenging Exmoor Beast. November is the finest time to visit. This may be one of the wettest places in the UK, but if it wasn't, it wouldn't look the way it does: deep, boggy peat moors, huge skyscapes under which ponies and red deer huddle, moss-laden elven oak and beech woods in sharp-sided gorges and always, always, plenty of rushing water.

The precision organisation of the Exmoor Beast makes great use of an out-of-season Butlins at Minehead as its base. As we're here on a different weekend (we hate people, remember?), there's no need for us to visit the chavtastic camp. Instead, we make our start in the rather more wonderful Dunster just up the road, ancestral home of the Luttrell family who, along with their contemporaries the Knights, colonised the moor with improbable farmsteads. When you ride over the Chains or Brendon Common past the ruins of such estates as Larkbarrow or Tom's Hill, the air of history hangs heavy in the air, as you realise

what an impossibly hard life those pioneering tenant farmers must have endured. Now, in the twenty-first century, with our four-wheel drives, instant electricity and global communications, we still regard these places as too inhospitable to live or work. It must have been a lot of fun in the blizzards of 1916, when 14 inches of snow cloaked Exmoor for weeks.

Let's make no bones about it: the Exmoor Beast is a beast. The hardest and longest climb is right at the beginning, where you take in about ten miles of climbing as soon as your tyres start going round. Going round more and more slowly in my case. Leaving Britain's trickiest main road, the A39, shortly before it tackles the infamous Porlock Hill, the road first rears up under a dense cover of gnarled branches in the thick mossy stillness of Horner Woods. As is his style, Phil quickly finds his rhythm on the steep slopes and rolls a gear on and up towards the landmark of Webber's Post, leaving me grunting and gasping in an effort to find a little more oxygen. The rutted roads are awash with water pouring down from the moor above after a number of heavy

Below: Carver Doone's old haunts. The legendary villain met his sticky end in a black mire somewhere on these wild tops.

Back on the main road above Porlock, we wind along a quick section of surprisingly flat well-surfaced tarmac with little traffic to bother us. It would be a different story on August Bank Holiday weekend, another good reason for heading here in November. Out of Somerset and into Devon: I know what's in front of us, and I don't want there to be any cars around. One of the country's fastest descents, Countisbury Hill.

Check brakes. Bump up and down just a little bit to check the tyres. Try not to think about spokes. Try not to think about potholes. Definitely don't think about crashing. The sea is down to the right; a long way down. We're

going to lose 1,000ft of height in a mile or so of descending, but if we go through one of those gateways on the right, we'll be losing 1,000ft in about 1,000ft. No bends to worry about, just point her and let her go.

Now, just as Phil goes uphill quicker than me, the same rule sees me descend the faster of the two of us. This changed a little bit when he got himself a better bike and better wheels, but generally, I will put a bit of daylight between us on a fast run, so I take the lead, all the better to see the tarmac in front of us. I don't use a bike computer (in fact I hate them – am I really only going at 15mph?) so I can't tell you exactly what

I clocked on Countisbury, but from previous experience and my clinical judgement, I would say I was somewhere between 60 and 70mph when I slapped on the Shimano anchors for the steepest bit at the bottom. This is 25 percent, and there's a bridge over the river into Lynmouth that feels like quite a corner at 60mph, so brakes aren't all bad.

Some people will tell you not to use the back brake too much as you might skid. Others will tell you that too much front brake will send you over the bars. While working for a professional team a few years ago, I got used to riding lots of different riders' bikes, often with the brakes

wired up the opposite way round. As a result, I got into the habit of always applying equal pressure to each brake and I can tell you that this technique has never let me down. Top tip. Write it down. That's yours to keep.

Still gurgling with laughter after the manic descent, and hoping the feeling in our fingers will soon return, we begin the beautiful but sapping drag out of Lynmouth. The coastal village and its larger twin Lynton on the cliff above are just a couple of minutes apart by cliff railway, but the main road joining the two that avoids the steepest slopes is fully six miles long.

Above: *Countisbury. Stay off the brakes if you dare as the road plunges 1,300ft in two miles.*

Lynton and Lynmouth are truly excellent places to be in June, when their annual community-led music festival takes place. A few years ago I drank lovely cheap local brews from the festival circuit's finest beer tent and watched Gruff Rhys in the park by the sea in Lynmouth, before jogging up the cliff path to see him join Charles Hazlewood for some experimental tomfoolery in Lynton Church directly afterwards. The whole place stops for music; it's a special weekend.

Lynmouth wasn't such a great place to be on 16 August 1952. The wettest August in memory culminated in a scarcely believable nine inches of rain in one night. The Chains, the area of bleak moorland dominating the western side of Exmoor, was already completely sodden, and every single drop that fell into the East Lyn, West Lyn, Hoaroak Water, Farley Water, Badgworthy Water, Oare Water and the myriad of little combes and valleys was going to end up at one single destination: Lynmouth. Debris, trees, boulders, all sorts, had built up against a bridge higher up the West Lyn which finally relinquished its grip on the banks and collapsed. Untold tons of water and matter hit the village in a tsunami of destruction that left 34 people dead and 420 homeless. Over 100 houses were destroyed. We pass a memorial where a whole row of cottages disappeared in a few tragic seconds that night. In such a small place, that's a tragedy of immense proportions.

Now we're climbing again. Across Brendon Common, across the Chains, on into the bleak interior of the moor. It's beautiful though, and the wind is no longer in our faces, so when it does rain, which it does, it's on our shoulders.

Left: The East Lyn and West Lyn were given a new course through Lynmouth after they destroyed the village in the flood of 1952.

Nothing as hard as this morning, but it's a long way up from the shores of the Bristol Channel to the source of the Exe. We're over the watershed, though: from here, everything drains to Exeter, rather than north to Lynmouth

One of the indisputable highlights of the Exmoor Beast is the fantastic ridge road that runs eastward along the southern uplands to Dulverton. With a wind on your back – it's not immense today, but I'm not complaining – you can fly along, crossing backwards and forwards across the county line. With the air blown clean by the storms, the views south are incredible. Dartmoor is almost touchable, and you can even catch a glimpse of the glittering Exe estuary as it spills into the English Channel. That's a long way.

I've been salivating for many miles at the prospect of a Dulverton sandwich, but it's not a good idea to eat too much. I'll only leave it on a Somerset hillside. It's too cold and wet to sit outside, and I don't want to be out here after dark, so we wolf it down and venture back on to the road, feet warmed by a radiator for ten minutes. Good job, as the last part, an uninspiring uphill drudge across the Brendon Hills to the east of the moor, is cold and wet.

Dunster. The castle. The old yarn market. More tearooms than people. Time for a phone call.

"Hi Dad, guess where I am."
"Ah! Did you go through Porlock?"
"It's just off the route, but not far."
"You didn't find my ball, then?"

Right: The River Barle, the River Exe's big brother, is the main waterway through the old hunting forest.

December

West Highland Way

I'm wet, I'm seriously annoyed, and I'm cold. Really cold. I think Phil is all of these things too, but we're not talking about it. We're also lost. It's dark. And it's Christmas. How on earth did it come to this?

"We should do something really big for December. Big finish. Crash, bang, fireworks, Christmas trees."

"Like a Tour of Lapland?"

"Hardly an iconic bike ride, is it?"

"Bethlehem and back?"

"Not snowy enough."

"The Alps again, then? Marmotte in winter?"

"Too snowy. The roads might be shut."

"Right, so you want snow, but not too much snow."

"Yeah."

"Somewhere in Scandinavia?"

"Ooh. Nice, but expensive. And we're back to the lack of iconicness issue again."

"Iconicness?"

"I know, shh. Hmm. Hmm. I've got it: the West Highand Way."

"That sounds hard. It's a footpath isn't it?"

"Glasgow to Ben Nevis. Well, it doesn't go up Ben Nevis exactly, it finishes at the bottom, in Fort William."

"Yeah, that sounds hard. Mountain bikes out again, then. How many days?"

"I was thinking one."

"One day? Glasgow to Ben Nevis? Isn't that about a hundred miles? Off road? In winter? You realise that it's daylight for about ten minutes up there at that time of year?"

"Oh yeah, that's brilliant! We should do it over the shortest day of the year as a night-day-night ride."

"Great."

Left: *Ascending the Devil's Staircase out of Glencoe on General Wade's old military road.*

It's so dark, I'm not even sure if we're on a path, let alone the right path.

I had always liked the idea of walking or riding the West Highland Way, heading north out of the Central Belt, into the mountains, the low road round Loch Lomond, Strathfillan, Glencoe, the Devil's Staircase. Following General Wade's eighteenth-century military roads, built to subdue the Jacobite Highlands, but famously only ever used by the Jacobites to march south and invade the Hanoverian lowlands and England. That sort of bitter irony would be enough to drive a King George mad.

Driving north-west up the A82, I'd often seen backpack-laden pilgrims following parallel routes, always heading in the same direction. Nobody seems to walk from Fort William to Glasgow, it's always the other way; symbolically leaving the grime and grunt of everyday life behind for the call of the mountains. I had daydreamed about riding it. It surely wouldn't be technically difficult. There wasn't a lot of tarmac around in 1700, of course, but these were

properly laid roads in their time, parts of the Way becoming traffic-free only when the A82 was rebuilt in the 1950s, allowing the masses access to the fabled North-West Highlands for the first time.

An enterprising endurance mountain biker I knew called Rob Lee had even ridden it there and back, non-stop. He might be a better bike rider than us, but if he could do that, we should be able to do it one-way, shouldn't we?

Grey light is finally beginning to show us where we are, or rather, where we aren't, which is on the West Highland Way. From Milngavie (I know that you say it "Millguy" thanks to an aggressive ex-girlfriend who grew up there – "MillGUY, ya stupit English basturt!") on the outskirts of Glasgow, we've traipsed north across the open country of the Campsie Fells, largely on hard fire trails, with our headlights as the only source of illumination for about two hours now. It has been very hard going on bumpy, slow paths, with frequent stops to check my aged map, purchased by parents many years ago

Above: Steps at Balmaha. Attempting the West Highland Way in one go in December means dealing with a lot of darkness.

Opposite: The falls at Glen Falloch are a roaring presence.

Above: Beinn Dorain
towers over the
route and the West
Highland Railway.

before ambitions were overtaken by common
sense and they began taking driving holidays
instead. In Christmas week, dawn in these
parts is around 9.15. It's now about 8.30 and
we can only just make out shapes of trees and
mountains against the sky. There's not a lot of
artificial light up here; even less at the top of our
journey, where we are scheduled to hit darkness
again tonight well short of our final target.

As far as I know, there aren't any long flights
of neatly cut steps on the West Highland Way.

That's how I know we're lost. The mountain
bikes, already heavy and cutting into our
shoulders so soon into our trek, are carried
down to the edge of Loch Lomond, the huge
expanse of water grey listless in the pre-dawn
murk. From here, the entire morning will be
spent upon the bonny, bonny banks, as we trace
the eastern shore of the great loch under the
slopes of Ben Lomond before emerging into the
vale of Strathfillan around lunchtime, we hope.
A few days ago, as we were packing up for the

trip, I thought I should give Rob Lee a call about our venture, see if he had any words of advice for us.

"Hey John, West Highland Way, then?"

"That's the plan, yes."

"Hardest thing I've ever done. I ought to go back and finish it some time."

realise I was no longer standing up. My friends had to bully me into giving up."

"Oh."

"The terrain was really technical for most of it, tricky enough walking. One bit along Loch Lomond must have been a four-mile carry. And I had to lower the bike, then me, off a ledge at one point."

Here, the old military road is our medium of transport, and will be until we reach Fort William or die trying. These roads and the town of Fort William itself are relics of the Jacobite rebellions and the suppression of them in the eighteenth century. General Wade took an army to build the network of roads to link the new forts after the rebellion of 1715, but it wasn't until Bonnie Prince Charlie's '45 uprising lay in tatters on the bloody moss of Culloden that Wade's successor, Caulfield, set about conquering Rannoch Moor with these stones. Ahead of us, this road will famously climb out of the enclosed steep sides of Glencoe via the zig-zags of the Devil's Staircase. We need to be over the top of there by 2pm to stand a chance of traversing the subsequent broken mountainside in daylight.

There are two important things you need to know about Glencoe:

a) The Glencoe Effect

Glencoe is massive. Really massive, hard for my feeble southern English brain to grasp. Buchaille Etive Mor, the giant Munro you turn away from to climb the Devil's Staircase, isn't even the biggest mountain in the glen. If you head on down the glen westward, it is tempting to park up and take a short walk across the valley floor and begin to scale one of the Three Sisters as they loom high above you. If you look again, you will see tiny toy bridges spanning the little stream flowing between you and the foot of the climbs, and strange tiny figures waddling across them. It is only then you realise the true size of the landscape you're in: that short walk would take an hour at least, the little stream is the gushing River Coe, and those figures are full grown men and women. You find yourself frowning like Dougal, while Father Ted holds up toy cows, saying, "These are close, those are far away." That is The Glencoe Effect in action.

b) The Glencoe Massacre

Before dawn on 13 February 1692, a fire was lit at Signal Rock in Glencoe. Billeted for the past fortnight with the MacDonalds of Glencoe, the local inhabitants, were a regiment of the army led by Campbells, fierce enemies of the MacDonalds for many years as a result of the latters' regular cattle-stealing raids on Campbell lands. The fire was the signal for the soldiers to rise up and put their hosts, man, woman and child, to the sword. The MacDonalds' chief, The MacIain, had been late in pledging allegiance to the crown, and this was the draconian price his clan would pay. 38 people died, many others escaping, sometimes with the assistance of soldiers horrified by what they had been asked to do. More are thought to have perished in the snow on the Devil's Staircase and other secret routes out of the glen as they hid from their would-be killers. Now, I'm not a particularly spiritual or mystical person, but I defy anybody, even those with no knowledge of this dark and shameful act, to walk under the high peaks of Glencoe in winter and not be somehow assailed with the knowledge that something bad once happened here.

Left: *General Wade's military roads were built to subjugate the Highlands, but were used by the Jacobites to invade the South.*

Next page: *Blizzard on the Devil's Staircase. A difficult time in the life of a cyclist.*

Above: *It is best not to photograph the photographer when he is this exhausted.*

When I puncture trying to skip a culvert that turned out to be wider than I thought, we are still a mile short of the bottom, and it's gone 2pm. Frozen fingers unravelling a fresh inner tube, I try to console myself by thinking of tighter spots that we've been in over the preceding 12 months. Not a good idea – there weren't any.

There's not much riding going on as we climb out of the glen. The snow on the ground is fresh and thick, and more is beginning to fall from the leaden sky, so the ride becomes a trudge. Each step forward results in a slide back of a few inches for the solid soles of our rugged mtb shoes. This in turn means the toes of our substantial neoprene overshoes gets tugged up and off the front of the shoe, leaving the thin leather and mesh unprotected against the

wet snow. After a mile of this I am deliriously considering a homespun amputation along the lines of Aron Ralston. My brain drifts off to an examination of films that are better watched in reverse, prompted by a friend's observation that, backwards, *127 Hours* becomes an uplifting tale of how a young disabled fellow finds a new arm in a cave. In *The Graduate*, Dustin Hoffman dumps his true love to embark on a steamy affair with her mother. In *Midnight Cowboy*, Jon Voigt recovers from his friend Hoffman's early death by leaving his life as a seedy stud in New York for a new life in the country. *Benjamin Button* is really, really boring.

The higher we get, the more the snow closes in. "The Buckle", as climbers call the great rock behind us, disappears into the grey and white

afternoon. There is no view over the top of the Staircase today. The weather has set in and the light is beginning to fail. Five miles of snowy mountainside separates us from Kinlochleven, the next lump of civilisation, and the next point where we've agreed to see Mark and the van.

"You need to be really careful on the descent from the Devil's Staircase to Kinlochleven," Rob Lee had told me the week before. "It's a lot further than it looks on the map, and it feels like there's just as much up as there is down."

"OK. You were all right on it, though?"

"I don't remember it at all. I was completely delirious at that point. The friend I was riding with said I was taking all sorts of risks and didn't know what I was doing."

Well, that's just great, then.

I won't forget that hour of slipping sideways through wet snow for a long time. There was a lot of clipping out, and then trying and failing to clip back in, as every time you put a foot down, your cleats got clogged with compacted snow. Fortunately, the snow seemed to give off its own ethereal light, reflecting what little was left in the sky, so we could still see what we were doing when we finally rolled down the fantastic fast chute next to the pipeline that leads down into Kinlochleven.å

Phil – Wet Wet Wet was a funny name for a band. But now I've spent some time trying to ride a bike and take photos in their home country, I have a finer understanding of their collective state of mind.

Water and cameras are generally not the best of friends and using your shiny new DSLR in the

__Above__: Pretending to be Sir Edmund Hillary with mountain bike.

rain and snow on the side of a mountain can cause some issues. Now, we're not talking about the gentle pitter-patter of a little light drizzle. We are talking a full-on hooley driving at every nook and cranny of your camera and your very being, trying to force its way in. So what can you do? Well, there are a few things I do:

1. Use a lens hood, it does help a bit.
2. Put the whole thing in a large clear plastic bag, zip-lock ones are best. You can cut a hole in the bag for the lens to poke out of and secure it with an elastic band. An additional hole for the viewfinder finishes it off. Better still, you can buy them already done from your local camera store. Less than a tenner and worth every penny.
3. Carry a lens cloth. Better still, carry two. You can't dry rain off the front of your lens with the sleeve of your fancy £200 Gore-tex jacket. I know, I've tried.
4. Question the sanity of trying to photograph cycling on the side of a Scottish mountain in the middle of December.

Mark had been amusing himself by taking photos of that part of Lochaber since we'd last seen him. He was particularly taken with the juxtaposition of some of Britain's most stunning scenery with some of Britain's most stunning cesspits. And we hadn't even reached

Fort William yet, the best illustration of the scenery–cesspit juxtaposition of all.

A hot drink, a sandwich, and we're ready to go. Sort of. The feel of the saddle on my wet, sore bum has a similar feeling to being hurled naked into a bath full of pebbles. Or perhaps that bit in Casino Royale where the baddie repeatedly thwacks a length of knotted rope into Bond's knackers.

It's proper dark now, and there is no snow on the ground at this lower elevation to add any light. There are still 12 miles of rough mountain country to cover before we emerge on to the road in Glen Nevis. However, surprisingly, this proves to be one of the ride's easier sections. The path is clear, well-trod, and doesn't go over any enormous mountains. The hefty Lochaber ridges and peaks shoulder each other for room against the inky sky, the bulk of the Mamore Forest massif pressing down on our shoulders as we keep the gear rolling through the darkness.

My difficulties now are all internal. Basically, I'm exhausted. We talked about packing up in Kinlochleven, but with neither of us wanting to be the one who called a halt to proceedings, we'd pressed on with fake bonhomie. So close to the finish, it would be a crying shame to give up now, but if you're going to die on a bike, you may as well be one mile from the end as 100. I thought again of Rob Lee, believing he was

Right: Following the old pipeline into Kinlochleven. Emerging from the snow is something of a relief.

standing up eating an energy bar chatting to his pals, when he was actually in a heap at their feet. A bit like falling asleep at the wheel on the M6, your actual view of the road replaced by a looped mental projection of it while your brain closes your eyes and tucks you in.

I thought of Tommy Simpson, Britain's only World Road Race Champion until the advent of Cavendish himself, begging to be put back on his bike on Mont Ventoux, moments before his death through exhaustion and heart failure. How far can you go? How much more can you take? This

is the real difference between great champions and good bike riders: the great champions don't know when to stop. I am neither a great champion nor a particularly good bike rider, and I feel that I should have stopped some time ago.

A weird thing happens: I haven't had a pee since before it got dark, yet I've drunk and drunk and drunk at every opportunity. When I finally decide to have one at one of our more and more frequent rest stops, I wee for what seems like a month or so. Like when you've had to wait for your girlfriend to have a shower the morning

Above: Night time in Glen Nevis, way behind schedule. Getting home for Christmas is the aim.

after you've had ten pints before collapsing on the sofa. Like if you stop weeing, something will come unravelled in the fabric of the universe. One of those wees, whereas, half a minute before I'd started, I didn't even want to go. Maybe it's the body demanding that you hang on to every last scrap of heat, energy and fluid.

There's not a lot of banter in this chapter. I think that tells its own story. Closer we come to where street lights pinken the sky ahead.

My thoughts begin to refocus slowly back to the things we've seen over these amazing 12 months. We're nearly done. And when we're done... what then? There's a euphoria tinged with a little empty hole at its centre, a weirdly wistful feeling.

It is very, very late at night. But here we are at last.

"Merry Christmas."
"Yeah. You too."

Below: Glen Nevis is one of Britain's darker corners at the 11th hour.

Next page: Christmas lights and frosty nights. A lovely end to 12 incredible months.

Acknowlegements

Words by John Deering
Photography by Phil Ashley
Original design by Jane Ashley

**Additional photography by John Deering, Jane and Emily Ashley
and Mark Langton.**

Thank you to everybody that has given us kit, fixed our bikes, fixed
our cars, made us food, made us laugh, ridden with us and drunk
with us. Thanks to those who occasionally took us seriously. Thanks
especially to Bob Johnson for lending us a load of his old junk.